Festivus! The Book

A Complete Guide to the Holiday for the Rest of Us

Mark Nelson

ISBN-13: 978-1511556392
ISBN-10: 1511556390

First Edition - 2015

Title: Festivus! The Book
A Complete Guide to the Holiday for the Rest of Us

Author: Nelson, Mark R., 1963-

Publication Information: Amazon Createspace
Subject Term: Holidays -- Humor
BISAC: Social Science / Holidays (non-religious)

818.607 NEL 2015   PN6231.H547 N46 2015

Dedicated to Mom and Dad

Table of Contents

Preface

The inaugural Festivus occurred in 1966 during the memorable first date of a young Daniel O'Keefe and his soon to be fiancé Deborah. How many people can recall a first date, other than the ones where they embarrassed themselves in an unfortunate bathroom accident? Something magical must have happened.

In what could be only considered the first Festivus Miracle, a new holiday was born that night. Throughout the 1970s and 80s in their Chappaqua, New York home, the O'Keefe family parents nurtured the growth of this strange annual occurrence. The legacy seems to have been significant, as it caused the holiday to be written into the annals of comedy history by the eldest son of the family and presented to the world in a 1997 episode of Seinfeld.

What is Festivus today? It should be noted that it still has no real connection to aquatic animals. Sure, the name Festivus can be connected to both fish and shellfish, but going into a zoology lesson would be akin to talking about the Pacific Northwest when one wanted to describe the first President of the United States... I lost my train of thought.

In the media, Festivus is often referred to as a "fake" holiday... surely because the person who writes the copy is a lazy news drone who used a thesaurus to change the word "parody" to "fake". Yes, when you saw Festivus on Seinfeld it was meant as a parody. However, when the holiday was celebrated in the O'Keefe family it was, as writer Dan O'Keefe puts it, "all too real."

Literally hundreds of thousands of people around the world view Festivus as a holiday worth embracing. The holiday's vast collection of celebrants are a diverse bunch, coming from all social and religious backgrounds. They are looking to have a laugh, celebrate Seinfeld, or poke fun at the commercial and religious aspects of the holiday season. They all celebrate Festivus as a holiday "For the Rest of Us". There is nothing fake about it. It's real and it's spectacular! ~ Mark Nelson

FESTIVUS

Festivus pole in the front yard of John M. Bunch, Tampa Florida.

Chapter 1 : **What's the Deal with Festivus?**

If you are reading this book, it might be safe to assume that you've heard of "Festivus". However, if you have picked up this tome in an effort to educate yourself about this strange new holiday, this book will become your Festivus bible.

Festivus is a secular holiday that was brought to the world through a single episode of the popular American sitcom *Seinfeld*. Originally aired in December 1997, the episode depicts a holiday that includes traditions such as erecting an unadorned aluminum pole, inviting family and friends to dinner, and airing grievances where you tell the others of all the ways they have disappointed you over the past year. After dinner, the "Feats of Strength" are performed, which involves wrestling the head of the household until he or she is pinned to the floor.

Since the airing of the original episode almost two decades ago, people around the world have adopted Festivus as a fun new tradition. Yes, it's true! People have actually decided to celebrate Festivus. Some are *Seinfeld* fans, who love everything about the groundbreaking series. They celebrate Festivus as an enjoyable tribute to *Seinfeld*. Others are folks who are disillusioned with Christmas, because of the commercial or religious aspects, or both. They celebrate Festivus as a fun way to protest.

In a fascinating turn, people have also embraced how Festivus was originally celebrated by the family of Dan O'Keefe, the writer credited for including Festivus in the *Seinfeld* episode. Since the original airing of the *Seinfeld*

version of Festivus, Dan has come forward to tell how his father, Daniel O'Keefe Sr., invented Festivus "out of the air", and how his own family once celebrated the offbeat holiday in an annual tradition.

In a tribute to Daniel O'Keefe's creation, people around the world are also beginning to incorporate the specific O'Keefe family traditions into their annual Festivus event.

Happy Festivus!

The first thing you should know is that the traditional greeting of Festivus is "Happy Festivus". Why Happy Festivus? Simply because this is how the characters in the *Seinfeld* episode "The Strike" greet each other.

In fact, almost every tradition we have about Festivus was originally devised by the writers of the popular 1990's situation comedy. It seems unbelievable that something that was written by a collection of relatively obscure television writers can carry so much credence almost 20 years later. In this case, it's the truth.

A Festivus for the Rest of Us!

"A Festivus for the rest of us," is the traditional slogan for Festivus, which has been taken to mean that Festivus is a secular holiday, with no religious or even social boundaries.

We first heard "a Festivus for the rest of us" on *Seinfeld*, when we witnessed Frank Costanza (actor Jerry Stiller) utter the phrase during the Festivus episode. When he explained Festivus to Kramer (Michael Richards), Frank exclaimed, "a Festivus for the Rest of Us!" coining a phrase to be used in popular culture for the next two decades and beyond. It should also be noted the phrase is often shortened by the rhyme, "Festivus Restivus."

The idea of something being for "the rest of us" has now spread throughout our society. For example, the phrase is now being used to describe a sport competition for the average person, inclusive college parties that don't abide by fraternal boundaries and holiday celebrations that don't include any religious connotations.

However, this is not the first time this phrase has ever been uttered. Apparently, when Frank Costanza's line was inserted into the episode's script, it was something writer Dan O'Keefe had once heard his own father utter in the past. On the occasion of the Festivus following his mother's passing, Daniel O'Keefe Sr., had referred to the day as "a Festivus for the rest of us."[1]

"A Festivus for the Rest of Us was an actual family Festivus motto," Dan O'Keefe has confirmed. "Referring initially to those remaining after the death of my father's mother, and then coming to mean in general a forward-looking focus on life and the living, i.e. 'Let the dead bury the dead'."[2]

Why the 23rd of December?

Festivus is celebrated annually on December 23rd. Many people often wonder how the official date for Festivus was derived. The short answer is that the date was chosen randomly by the *Seinfeld* writers.

December 23

In the *Seinfeld* episode "The Strike", when Kramer approaches his boss at the bagel shop to ask for a day off for Festivus, he states, "Listen Harry, I need the 23rd off." It was at this point that the date for the *Seinfeld* Festivus was established.

There is further evidence in the episode to support the notion of Festivus being on the 23rd. Later, in the scene at the diner, Kramer made the announcement, "It's a big dinner, Tuesday night at Frank's house. Everybody's coming." In looking back, December 23rd in the year the episode was released was in fact a Tuesday. Apparently, there was due diligence applied to the scriptwriting, and December 23rd was in fact meant as the official date.

In a 2009 online chat through the *Washington Post*, writer

Dan O'Keefe was asked if there was any significance in "23 December". He confirmed that the date was chosen "randomly".[3]

Incidentally, the real Festivus, as celebrated by the O'Keefe family was not celebrated on the 23rd. "It didn't really have a set date. Which made it more ominous. It was a floating holiday," Dan O'Keefe has said.[4]

The notion of a "pop-up" Festivus remains somewhat true even today, as many people do not actually celebrate Festivus on December 23rd. They might celebrate on a more convenient day in December, or even at another time of the year.

Still this date remains the center of modern Festivus activity, especially in popular culture and the media, even though many folks take the liberty of celebrating Festivus any day they please. The very nature of the holiday allows for freedom.

Chapter 2 : The Seinfeld
Story of Festivus

We cannot go any further in our discussion of Festivus without an in-depth review of the main source of the holiday's traditions. The Seinfeldian origins of Festivus can be dated back to the 9th season *Seinfeld* episode titled "The Strike". Nearly every nuance of all *Seinfeld*-based Festivus traditions are found in this episode.

Let us begin...

Near the beginning of the episode, it was revealed how George's family had celebrated a strange holiday named "Festivus". Apparently, Jerry had known about it, but when George received a Festivus card from his father, Elaine was made aware of the holiday as well. This resulted in Elaine teasing George, which caused him to run off, upset and embarrassed. This was our initial introduction to Festivus, and of course, illustrating how upsetting Festivus was for George Costanza.

Later, at Jerry's apartment, Jerry and Elaine teased George by wishing him a "Happy Festivus". Kramer overheard this, and being forever curious about anything inane and wacky, he contacted Frank Costanza to learn more about Festivus.

Frank met Kramer at the bagel shop where Kramer was working. This was the moment when we witnessed how Frank expressed concern over the increased commercialism and consumerism that tended to saturate the December holiday season. Frank also told the tale of a routine outing to secure a Christmas gift for his son, which resulted in a fight over a doll. This was the exact moment when Frank came to the realization that there should be a new holiday:

> **Frank Costanza**: *Many Christmases ago, I went to buy a doll for my son. I reached for the last one they had, but so did another man. As I rained blows upon him, I realized there had to be another way.*

Kramer asked Frank whether Festivus had a Christmas tree. Frank then told Kramer about the "unadorned aluminum pole" he had conceived as his symbol of Festivus, and how he "finds tinsel distracting".

Kramer's interest in Festivus caused Frank to decide that it was time to resurrect the tradition. Frank then rushed off to make preparations, most importantly to fetch his aluminum pole from the crawlspace.

To George's dismay, he soon discovered that Festivus had made a comeback. This occurred when George and Jerry were in Monk's Diner, and Frank arrived dragging his aluminum pole, accompanied by the instigator, Kramer, in tow. When George discovered that his father had resurrected Festivus and was planning a dinner at his place, he had a meltdown. Frank tried to inspire George by playing a cassette tape that was recorded at a past Festivus, but this only caused George to sit, head in hands and moan in pain. At the end of the scene, George rushed out of the diner yelling, "No Feats of Strength. I hate Festivus."

Meanwhile, in a parallel story line, George had used Festivus as a defensive excuse with his boss, Mr. Kruger. George had been confronted by Kruger after handing out cards to his fellow employees stating a donation had been made to a fake charity George invented named "The Human Fund" with its slogan "Money For People". The lie had been furthered by Kruger himself, when he had donated $20,000 of company money to the Human Fund. Once Kruger had become aware of the ruse, he confronted George, who defended himself by giving the excuse that he feared persecution for his belief in Festivus. Attempting to call his bluff, Kruger then forced George to verify his excuse by inviting him to witness Festivus at the Costanza residence.

Kramer, who was also invited to the Festivus celebration, asked for time off from his bagel vendor job. When his boss told him he could not get time off for Festivus, he decided to go on strike. Kramer was then shown marching on the street in front of the bagel shop in a one man picket line with a sign that read "Festivus yes! Bagels no!"

In the final part of the episode, we see the Festivus dinner at the Costanza residence. George was the first to arrive with his boss, Mr. Kruger. As soon as George introduced Kruger to his father, Frank Costanza insisted on showing Kruger the aluminum pole which had been erected on one side of the dining room. Frank explained how the pole had a "very high strength-to-weight ratio", to which Kruger replied, "I find your belief system fascinating."

Jerry and Elaine arrived next. Elaine's hair was still moist and flat from an impromptu steam bath she received at the bagel shop, after a defiant Kramer sabotaged a pipe which burst and filled the bagel shop with steam. Her mascara had also run, making her eyes look very dark.

Once Kramer arrived, everyone was surprised to see he had brought two bookies from an off-track betting location... men that Elaine was attempting to avoid. Kramer explained how the bookies had been looking for Elaine, and now they had found her, and therefore declared the reunion to be a Festivus Miracle!

Finally, dinner was served. As the guests were being seated, Estelle Costanza brought the main course to the table, which is best described as a plate of sliced meatloaf on a bed of lettuce.

Once everyone was seated, Frank announced that it was time for the Airing of Grievances:

> **Frank Costanza:** *The tradition of Festivus begins with the airing of grievances. I got a lot of problems with you people. Now you're going to hear about it.*

Frank began by telling Kruger that his company stinks. However, when he attempted to go into more detail he suddenly lost his train of thought. Frank's vague attempt to air a grievance against Kruger is the only grievance that was heard.

Then, to Jerry's surprise, his girlfriend Gwen arrived. Since Jerry had been trying to avoid her, he asked how she knew where he was. Kramer interrupted by explaining that he was the one who informed Gwen of Jerry's whereabouts. Kramer brazenly declared this to be another Festivus Miracle, making Jerry scowl.

Frank then announced that it was time for the Feats of Strength:

> **Frank Costanza:** *And now, as Festivus rolls on, we come to the Feats of Strength.*

Initially, Frank appointed Kramer as the person who would wrestle. However Kramer conveniently remembered he had to work a double-shift at the bagel shop, as his self-imposed strike had ended prematurely.

Everybody around the table then wondered who would be required to do the Feats of Strength. As Kruger took a drink of liquor from a flask he replied, "How 'bout George." That settled it! Frank decided that he would wrestle his own son. He then informed the gathering that Festivus would not end until George had pinned him:

> **Frank Costanza:** *Until you pin me George, Festivus is not over.*

In preparation, Frank removed his cardigan, and then he uttered, "Let's rumble!"

The story of the *Seinfeld* Festivus ended with the camera outside the Costanza residence, slowly panning away. We could still hear the voices of the Costanza family inside:

> **Estelle***: I think you can take him Georgie.*
> **George***: Come on, be sensible!*
> **Frank***: Stop crying and fight your father.*

The Main Elements of a Seinfeld Festivus

The *Seinfeld* episode "The Strike" revealed the Festivus celebration includes four main components:

The Festivus Pole
The Costanza's tradition began with an unadorned aluminum pole, which Frank praised for its "very high strength-to-weight ratio". The pole was chosen apparently in opposition to the commercialization of highly decorated Christmas trees, because it is "very low-maintenance". The pole remains unadorned because the holiday's patron, Frank Costanza, "finds tinsel distracting".

The Festivus Dinner
Festivus included a family dinner. Traditionally, this is an important part of Festivus as it is the time when you gather your family together for the airing of grievances. The traditional Costanza-style meal is meatloaf, served on a bed of lettuce. There is no drinking, except liquor from a flask.

The Airing of Grievances
At the beginning of the Festivus dinner, each participant tells friends and family how they've disappointed them in the past year. As stated by Frank Costanza, "I've got a lot of problems with you people. Now you're going to hear about it!"

The Feats of Strength
After dinner, the head of the household tests his or her strength against one participant he or she chooses. Festivus is not considered over until the head of the family has been pinned. However, a participant may be allowed to decline to attempt to pin the head of the household if they have something better to do instead.

oddly decorated vague
curious O'Keefe childrentinfoil
experimenting **Deborah** Reader's Digest
Samuel Beckett Krapp's Last Tape
create a holiday that was just for his family bizarre
Are we Getting Along, or Are We Getting On?
wasn't beholden to anything political or religious

cassette recorder M&Ms
lick plates **randomly occur** ham clock and a bag

Daniel Lawrence O'Keefe
Daniel
O'Keefe
Viking helmet

Fuck Fascism

turkey dinner hats Life... Is Like a Fountain
original tradition **Play-Doh** Billy Joel's Greatest Hits

flaunt the laws of etiquette
beef stew **O'Keefe family** dunce cap
talk with mouth full awful Irish death music
Are we too easily made Glad? **Are we Scared? Yes!**

listen to the tapes Dan O'Keefe
clock Chappaqua
tapes **clock in a bag** theme

That's not for you to know!
Willie Nelson's Stardust American flag bag
family celebration
pulled the name out of the air

Larry Dan New York
lamb chops
chocolate kisses Festivus

The Real Festivus gripe
audio recordings first date Mark
tape recordings no set date
pecan pie
Pepperidge Farm
music not celebrated at Christmas-time
unilaterally decided the original Festivus
annual tradition turkey
Are we Depressed? Yes!
clock in a bag
complain champagne

Chapter 3 : The O'Keefes
(The Real Festivus)

Now that we have seen how Festivus occurred on *Seinfeld*, let us turn the clock back to a time when Festivus actually began.

People may be unaware that before Festivus appeared in *Seinfeld*, it had actually been celebrated in the household of a Chappaqua, New York family by the surname of O'Keefe.

Yes! Festivus did actually exist in the O'Keefe family long before it was in the *Seinfeld* series. It was only made a part of *Seinfeld* when writer Dan O'Keefe included aspects of his family's Festivus tradition in a *Seinfeld* episode. (More about that in the next chapter.) In 2005, Dan O'Keefe would even go on to publish the book *The Real Festivus*, a fascinating tell-all look into his family's annual tradition.

Festivus was invented by Dan's father, Daniel Lawrence O'Keefe, a writer who worked as an editor at *Reader's Digest*. It was in 1966, when he unilaterally decided he wanted a special new holiday for himself. Dan O'Keefe would later describe his father's original intention which was to, "create a holiday that was just for his family, that wasn't beholden to anything political or religious".[5]

How did Daniel come up with the name "Festivus"? According to Dan O'Keefe, his father "pulled the name out of the air". Daniel O'Keefe Sr. sometimes alluded to the fact that Festivus meant "party" in Latin, however the curious O'Keefe children searched, and they could never find a reference to "Festivus" in any books.

For the O'Keefes, Festivus was a family celebration. It

was generally celebrated solely within the O'Keefe family, which consisted of parents (Daniel and Deborah) plus three sons, Daniel (Danny), Lawrence (Larry) and Markham (Mark).

Clearly, the creativity gene is dominant in the O'Keefe family. The youngest son, Mark O'Keefe, went on to become a comedy screenwriter, most famous for writing and producing the Jim Carey film *Bruce Almighty* and the Adam Sandler comedy *Click*. Middle child, Larry O'Keefe, is now a renowned composer and lyricist for Broadway musicals, film and television. The eldest son, Dan O'Keefe is currently a writer and producer, best known for his writing on *Seinfeld*, *The Tonight Show with Jay Leno*, *The Drew Carey Show*, *The League*, *Married* and the current HBO hit *Silicon Valley*.

The O'Keefe Festivus celebrations spanned from the time Daniel and Deborah O'Keefe were engaged, through the time when their sons grew up, until the time that the boys left the house to go out on their own. In his book, Dan O'Keefe alludes to the fact that he assumed his parents continued to celebrate Festivus even after the children had grown and left the house.

So what was the real Festivus like? If you thought the original Festivus involved an aluminum pole and feats of strength you might be surprised. It didn't. The real Festivus was even more bizarre.

For starters, the real Festivus was not celebrated at Christmas-time. It didn't have a set date and it could randomly occur anytime of the year. There was no rule or pattern to its occurrence. The O'Keefe siblings never knew when Festivus would happen. Dan O'Keefe has memories of coming home from school and discovering the house candlelit and oddly decorated. This was how he knew it was time for Festivus.

To the O'Keefe boys the origin and meaning of Festivus was always vague. They often wondered if it was some sort of throwback to college fraternity days, or even joked that their father was probably experimenting on them. At one point their parents actually admitted that the first Festivus occurred on their first date in 1966. Over time, the boys also came to understand that their mother knew something about the meaning of Festivus, but she kept it to herself. The true meaning of Festivus seemed like an inside joke to which only the parents were privy.

One of the main elements of the O'Keefe Festivus were tape recordings. The idea of recording Festivus proceedings on audiotape came from the play *Samuel Beckett Krapp's Last Tape*, the story of an aged bitter man who listens to tapes of himself as a middle-aged man, who is in turn listening and commenting on tapes made when he was a young man. It was like the Droste effect (the effect of a picture appearing within itself), but on audio tape. Apparently, Daniel O'Keefe Sr. had taken a liking to the idea of audio recordings that could be reviewed in future sessions.

Thus Daniel O'Keefe Sr. taped most of the O'Keefe Festivus celebrations on his cassette recorder. In fact, the tapes still exist, and are part of the O'Keefe family collection. Because the tapes were such an integral part of the O'Keefe Festivus, this is one of the original traditions that was actually included in the *Seinfeld* version of the holiday.

The first official Festivus that included the O'Keefe children was held in 1975. They ate a big turkey dinner and afterwards

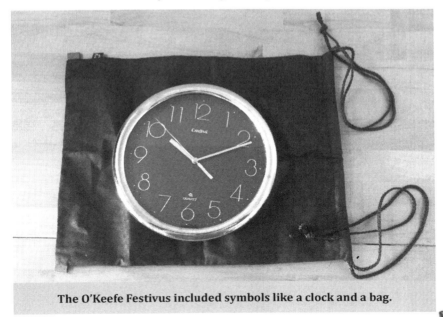

The O'Keefe Festivus included symbols like a clock and a bag.

they looked at family photos. There was no aluminum pole or feats of strength, but there was an O'Keefe version of the "airing of grievances". At the end of the evening, the family members all took turns telling the tape recorder about their past year.

The O'Keefe Festivus had symbols and props which weren't in the *Seinfeld* version of the holiday. For example, one of the main symbols of the holiday was a "clock and a bag", and sometimes a clock "in" a bag. The significance of the bag and the clock was unknown. Apparently, when the O'Keefe siblings would ask about the meaning, Daniel O'Keefe Sr. would simply reply, "That's not for you to know!" How mysterious!

There were no costumes for Festivus, however hats were often worn. Some of the favorites were a Viking helmet (with Play-Doh horns affixed), a brimless Cub Scout cap (including tinfoil adornments) or a pointy dunce cap. These were typical accoutrements manufactured by a gang of creative youths.

Daniel O'Keefe Sr.'s favorite Festivus symbol was a sign that simply said "Fuck Fascism". Of course, Deborah O'Keefe didn't like the notion of the expletive, and Daniel was convinced to alter the sign so it read "Screw Fascism". However, by the next year it was back to the old version with the original sentiment. Daniel was a confirmed liberal and certainly didn't mind sharing his disdain for the right-wing. This was also evidenced by the fact that he gleefully celebrated the anniversary of Richard Nixon's resignation.

As part of the annual Festivus tradition, Daniel O'Keefe would also bring out his American flag and place it on the flagpole mounted on the upstairs porch. Actually, the

Oddly enough, the clock would sometimes be put in the bag and then nailed to the wall. Why? That's not for you to know!

flag was a tradition in the O'Keefe family and was displayed on the Fourth of July and Memorial Day as well. The flag also made an appearance at other important family events such as birthdays, anniversaries, Thanksgiving, and even on occasions celebrating good report cards. Marking important days was a tradition in the O'Keefe household.

The O'Keefe Festivus celebration would begin with a musical performance and follow with dinner and gifts. In *The Real Festivus*, Dan O'Keefe describes his family's Festivus music as "awful Irish death music". Dan actually suggests that you listen to music that is "related to your particular ethnicity". As well, he suggests that you listen to albums such as Willie Nelson's *Stardust* or Billy Joel's *Greatest Hits*, just as his family loved to do.

As the party progressed to dinner, the table was usually decorated with chocolate kisses, candies and any other knickknacks that seemed appropriate. Occasionally each place setting had a small container of Play-Doh, and the diners were expected to mold it into some sort of object. After each person's creativity was expressed in colored dough, the creations were judged by Deborah O'Keefe.

It was traditional for the adults to drink champagne, while the entire family feasted upon a main course of turkey, ham, beef stew or lamb chops. Dan O'Keefe describes Festivus dinner as the one time when his family was able to flaunt the laws of etiquette. Family members would freely be able to lick their plates, talk with their mouths full and interrupt each other without repercussions. Surely, this was all done to their mother's chagrin.

In his book, O'Keefe describes pecan pie for dessert. However, in interviews he has also alluded to a Pepperidge Farm brand cake, which was a fixture at most family celebrations. When asked about the cake Dan O'Keefe explained, "My Mom would take a Pepperidge Farm cake, usually a yellow cake with chocolate frosting, and stud the exterior with M&Ms. Not just for Festivus, but for birthdays, the 4th of July and other holidays."

There were gifts, but just a few. The boys would wrap household items and give them to their parents. For example, rolls of toilet paper, forks and knives, books (even the ones their father was in the process of reading) and rocks and sticks from the yard even made an appearance as Festivus gifts. The parents also gave gifts to the children, however they were always gag gifts such as a camera that squirted water, or a garbage can featuring the faces of all the Presidents, which included Richard Nixon's face in a larger oval as he was the current President at the time the can was manufactured.

Finally, the family would gather in the living room and listen to the tapes from previous Festivus celebrations, and then they would record the current year's diatribe. Each member of the family would take turns speaking into the tape recorder. Although this part of the holiday mirrored Frank Costanza's "Airing of Grievances", it was never officially labeled as such. The moniker Airing of Grievances was solely part of the *Seinfeld* version of Festivus.

A tape recorder was a huge part of the O'Keefe Festivus.

All members of the family participated. First Daniel O'Keefe Sr. spoke. His grievances were usually directed toward work. Then, Deborah O'Keefe would take her turn. She would also complain about her work as an English professor, sometime focusing on student projects. Finally, the children would be asked to take their turns. They would grumble about bullies at school and their teachers. However, other than gripes, the tape recordings also recorded pleasantness, such as memories of vacations, and recollections of promotions, anniversaries, family visits and other happy events. It wasn't all bad news, as the happy times were put on record as well. Dan O'Keefe and his siblings still have the tapes and they seem to be a valuable, if not arcane, record of family history. Several transcripts of the tapes are also included in *The Real Festivus*.

As a lark, the O'Keefe boys would sometimes manufacture dunce caps to wear at Festivus.

Most O'Keefe Festivus celebrations had a theme, though the stated theme was often too vague to be of any real meaning to the celebrants. For example, some of the stated themes were "Are we Scared? Yes!", "Are we Depressed? Yes!", "Are we too easily made Glad?", "Are we Getting Along, or Are We Getting On?" and "Life... Is Like a Fountain." Daniel O'Keefe Sr. devised the themes and he usually didn't tell the celebrants much about what he was intending as a message. The vagueness of the theme seemed to be part of the holiday. There is a complete list of the Festivus themes in *The Real Festivus*. Check it out for additional Festivus-style vagueness.

In the conclusion of his book, Dan O'Keefe refers to his family's Festivus as, "heartwarmingly peculiar and occasionally, peculiarly heartwarming." If you haven't read his book, I suggest you get a copy of it. It's not currently in print so you may have to buy a used copy or find one at your local library. If you are a true Festivus aficionado, it is strongly suggested that you endeavor to locate and read this definitive work.

Despite the mysterious nature of its many traditions, the main theme of the "Real Festivus" was always family. In 1997, when Dan O'Keefe explained "Festivus" to the other *Seinfeld* writers, this must have been very clear, as the *Seinfeld* version of the holiday certainly carries this motif forward.

In 2004, when Daniel O'Keefe Sr. was informed by a writer from the New York Times that his holiday was catching on, his reply was, "Have we accidentally invented a cult?"[6]

Sadly, on 29 August 2012 at the age of 84, Daniel O'Keefe Sr. passed away. Though he is gone, it seems like his strange holiday will be remembered for some time to come, as Festivus grows in popularity every year. How bizarre is that? Daniel would have loved it! Daniel O'Keefe, we thank you for the holiday for the rest of us.

It may not be Pepperidge Farm, but the author has studded a homemade cake with M&M's in the same style as an O'Keefe celebration cake.
Are we Scared? Yes!

Remember "The O'Keefes"? (2003)

In 2003, Mark O'Keefe, the youngest member of the O'Keefe clan, created and wrote a television sitcom for the *WB Network* called *The O'Keefes*.

Originally titled "Brave New World", *The O'Keefes* was billed as a "semi-autobiographical" comedy. Just like the real O'Keefes, the fictitious O'Keefe family consisted of parents (Harry and Ellie) plus three children (Danny, Lauren and Mark). They may have made the middle child a girl, but they didn't sway too far from the names of the actual O'Keefe children.

From the original *WB Network* press release: "This new half-hour family comedy series takes a humorous look at our so-called 'normal' society through the eyes of one not-so-normal family as they try to keep their own unique values alive in a world where conformity rules."

A main plot point was how the children were home-schooled by their quirky parents. Also, one of the nuances was how the father added a special addendum to the daily Pledge of Allegiance that served to address many of the ills that plague modern life.

In the series, the O'Keefe family rejected many of society's conventions and created many family traditions that were patently their own. For example, rather than celebrating each person's birthday individually, the father (played by Judge Reinhold) created a unique annual family celebration known as the "Festival of Birth."

Does this sound familiar? Of course it does. Unfortunately, Episode 6, which was the actual episode titled "Festival of Birth" never aired, as the show was prematurely cancelled. We are left wondering what quirkiness Mark O'Keefe might have revealed in that particular episode.

Would television watchers have had another example of O'Keefe family folklore to admire?

Comparing the Festivi

Now that we've discussed the *Seinfeld* Festivus and the "Real Festivus", let's make a comparison of their specific traditions.

	Seinfeld Festivus... a la "The Strike"	The "Real Festivus"... a la The O'Keefes
Dinner	Meatloaf. No liquor, except liquor from a flask.	Turkey, ham or lamb chops. Champagne for the adults. Pepperidge Farm cake with M&M decorations for dessert. Place settings feature chocolate kisses & Play-Doh for the children.
Festivus Pole	An unadorned aluminum pole with high strength-to-weight ratio.	No Festivus pole.
Airing of Grievances	You tell everyone how they've disappointed you in the past year.	You complain about work, school and anything else... into a tape recorder.
Feats of Strength	The head of the household is pinned.	No Feats of Strength.
Gifts	No gifts were exchanged in the *Seinfeld* episode.	Crazy, gag gifts were exchanged. A form of regifting occurred.
Decorations	No tinsel.	The O'Keefe children adorned home-made party hats with tin foil. The national flag is flown. Political signs were displayed.
Music	None shown.	Music pertaining to your ethnicity, or if you prefer, Willie Nelson's "Stardust" or Billy Joel's "Greatest Hits".
Theme	No special theme.	Each Festivus was assigned a vague theme. e.g. "Are we too easily made glad?"

Does Dan O'Keefe Still Celebrate Festivus?

In the next chapter, you will read how television writer Dan O'Keefe Jr. was coerced into including Festivus in an episode of *Seinfeld*. However, before we go on, let's answer the question: "Does Dan O'Keefe still celebrate Festivus?"

A bit of advice for all "door-to-door aluminum pole salespeople" out there: stay away from Dan O'Keefe's home. When asked if he currently celebrates Festivus in his own household, Dan quickly replied, "Oh, hell no!"

Yes, despite being responsible for releasing his father's holiday on the world, Dan O'Keefe vehemently avoids Festivus himself.

Still, Dan appears to be the present day spokesperson for Festivus, as he is routinely asked to give interviews to the media on the topic. When asked about this, Dan responded by making a point of explaining that he only speaks to media outlets that regularly contact him with Festivus-related questions. He doesn't go out of his way to expound Festivus to the masses. "I have no current participation in it," he said. "If the media asks me a question, I try to answer it."

If you've ever seen Dan giving a television interview, you likely noticed how he plays the role of the consummate comedian, always seeking a punchline. Dan loves to apply his offbeat sense of humor to most Festivus-related topics. However, that's as far as he takes it.

Dan continues to work as a writer and producer in the television industry. When asked if he ever thought about writing "Festivus" into any of his current TV projects, even as a one-line sendup to the holiday, or maybe slipping an aluminum pole surreptitiously in the corner of a set, he repeated his response of, "Oh hell no!" Seems definite, doesn't it?

Do you recall in "The Strike" when George Costanza ran out of the diner saying, "No feats of strength. I hate Festivus!" Always remember, Dan is credited with writing that script.

The Strike

Schvitz

Rained Blows

Doll Shopping

Tinsel

Gwen

Feminist

Unadorned Studio 54 with a Menorah OTB

Captain Nemo Let's Rumble Distracted

Feats of Strength

Seinfeld

Head of the Household

Pepperidge Farm

Festivus Dinner

Train of Thought Money for People

Crawlspace

A Festivus for the Rest of Us

Festivus Miracle

Flask Not the Feats of Strength

Tape Recorder

Costanza Meatloaf

Festivusite Two Bookies Submarine Captain

23 December

Pinned PBR

Festivus

Strength-to-Weight Ratio

Silk Sheet Dan O'Keefe Fake Phone Number

Pulling a Whatley Seinfeldist

Happy Festivus Georgie Yamahama Cassette Tapes

Wagner Pole Kruger Industrial Smoothing Beer Can Festivus Pole

Clock Airing of Grievances

Newcomers Kruger O'Keefe

Aluminum Human Fund

Sawbuck

Happy Festivus

Seinfeldism Daniel Von Bargen Two-face

18 December 1997 Cloning Sheep No Bagel

Festivus Restivus

Spaghetti Belief System Denim Vest

Chapter 4 : "The Strike"

We now fast forward from the 1970s/80s in Chappaqua, New York to 1997 in Los Angeles, California, where Dan O'Keefe Jr. was now working as a writer for the *Seinfeld* series. He had already successfully written a few episodes, such as "The Blood" *(S09E04)* and "The Pothole" *(S08E16)*, and he had contributed to several other episodes. However, sitcom writers always had to be on the hunt for fresh ideas. It was a never-ending cycle, and writers often drew from their own personal experiences to form ideas for future scripts.

At the outset, Dan O'Keefe didn't consider his family's quirky Festivus holiday as an idea worth sharing. Dan recalls his initial feelings, "I did not pitch Festivus as an episode. In fact I had totally blocked it out of my mind."[7]

To Dan's surprise, his youngest brother Mark let it slip to a few of his *Seinfeld* co-writers that their family celebrated a weird holiday named "Festivus". The other writers thought it was funny enough for the series, however Dan was not so sure. "I fought against it," O'Keefe told *Mother Jones* magazine in 2013.[8]

However the other *Seinfeld* writers, relentless in their hunt for a comedy angle, forced Dan to spill all the details of his family Festivus. As Dan recalls, he was "dragged into it against my will by Alec Berg, Jeff Schaffer and Dave Mandel, who literally sat me down and refused to let me leave a diner until I agreed to write it into an episode."[9]

Once Dan had finally told the story of Festivus, "They were just speechless due to the sheer oddity of it". However, they unanimously came to the conclusion, "This needs to be on television, the story needs to be told."[10]

Dan still continued to think that a Festivus story arc would be embarrassing and drag the show down. However, it turned out that Jerry Seinfeld also took a liking to the idea and that made it official. Festivus was then written into the episode "The Strike". There was no turning back.

"The Strike"

Release Date: 18 December 1997

Episode No: Season 9 Episode 10

Production Code: 910

Running Time: 21:53

Episode Synopsis

When an increase in the minimum wage finally meets the 12-year-old demands of the striking employees of H&H Bagels, Kramer announces that he's going back to work. Meanwhile, at Tim Whatley's Hanukkah party, Jerry meets what he considers an attractive woman. However, later when he meets her for another date she seems far less attractive to him. With the encouragement of Kramer, Frank Costanza decides to resurrect Festivus, a holiday he invented and has celebrated in the past. Elaine has been using a fake phone number she gives to men she finds undesirable. However, it backfires on her when she writes the number on a card that will entitle her to a free submarine sandwich... and she needs the card back. George gives away fake donation cards as Christmas gifts at work, however Mr. Kruger, George's boss, discovers the ruse. George uses "Festivus" as an excuse, and as a result he has to bring Kruger to his family's Festivus celebration to prove that the zany holiday actually does exist.

Cast and Crew

Directed by: Andy Ackerman

Writers: Dan O'Keefe, Alec Berg and Jeff Schaffer

Cast:

- Jerry Seinfeld: Jerry Seinfeld
- Julia Louis-Dreyfus: Elaine Benes
- Michael Richards: Cosmo Kramer
- Jason Alexander: George Costanza
- Jerry Stiller: Frank Costanza
- Estelle Harris: Estelle Costanza
- Bryan Cranston: Tim Whatley
- Daniel von Bargen: Mr. Kruger
- Karen Fineman: Gwen
- Dave Florek: Harry
- Kevin McDonald: Denim Vest
- Tracy Letts: Counterguy
- Amit Itelman: Employee
- Stacey Herring: Sandy
- Colin Malone: Sleazy Guy
- Jerry Dixon: Customer

Production Trivia

The cast and crew of *Seinfeld* first assembled to read "The Strike" on Thursday, November 20, 1997.

The normal production schedule was accelerated so that the crew would be free to celebrate the Thanksgiving holiday on the 27th. The exterior scenes were filmed on Sunday the 23rd, with additional scenes filmed the following afternoon. The remainder of the episode was filmed in front of a live studio audience the following night.[11]

It is said that it took eight hours to shoot the complex Festivus dinner scene.[12]

Shooting Locations

- The episode was taped at CBS Studio Center - 4024

Radford Avenue, Studio City, Los Angeles, California.

- Exterior scenes of the Off Track Betting location were filmed at 164 Court Street, Brooklyn, New York.

- The exterior of La Bonite en Bois restaurant (where Jerry meets Tim Whatley and Gwen) was shot at 75 West 68th Street, New York.

References to other Seinfeld Episodes

- Near the beginning of the episode, when Jerry meets Gwen, he introduced himself as, "Hi. I'm Jerry. You might not know it to look at me, but I can run really, really fast." This was likely a reference to the Season 6 episode "The Race" *(S06E10)*.

- At the Costanzas', Mr. Kruger recognized Kramer as Dr. Van Nostrand. This was a reference to the earlier season 9 episode "The Slicer" *(S09E07)*, when Kramer, who was dressed in his butcher's smock, posed as a dermatologist doing a skin cancer screening. *(Also see "Notable Goofs")* Incidentally, "Dr. Van Nostrand" is also the name of an unseen character referred to several times in the 1963 *Alfred Hitchcock Hour* episode "The Dark Pool" *(S01E29)*. Coincidence? We think not.

- Other Christmas related *Seinfeld* episodes were "The Red Dot" *(S03E12)*, "The Pick" *(S04E13)* and "The Race" *(S06E10)*.

- The episode that aired prior to "The Strike" was "The Apology". The episode that followed was "The Dealership".

Notable Goofs

Every television episode has a few goofs, and "The Strike" is no exception...

- Jerry stated that Gwen "looks good when sitting in the back booth" at the coffee shop, and that he'll try to always sit there with her. However, on the two subsequent occasions that they ate there, they just sat in the booth that is directly behind the cash register, and not actually in the back booth.

- Elaine is a rule breaker! Who knew? When she is at the Off-

Track Betting location, there is a sign on the window that states, "No verbal bets. Cash must accompany betting slip." However, she places a verbal bet for a race at Belmont, without any paperwork.

- When Elaine looks down at Kramer's business card from 10 years ago, the card says "Cosmo Kramer Bagel Technician". If the card was printed 10 years earlier, why would it have his first name? Kramer never used his first name and kept it secret from everyone until more recently in the series.

- When Kramer returned to work at H&H Bagels, he claimed he had never seen a raisin bagel before. However, previously in the 8th season episode "The Muffin Tops", he served pizza bagels made from cinnamon raisin bagels to the patrons of his "Peterman Reality Bus Tour".

- Since Mr. Kruger had already acknowledged Kramer as "Dr. Van Nostrand", why wasn't he suspicious when Frank Costanza referred to Kramer as "Mr. Kramer"?

- Earlier in the episode, Frank had expressed derision for tinsel. However at the dinner, as he is introducing Mr. Kruger to the aluminum pole, a garland of tinsel was clearly visible on the wall in the background. Maybe Estelle put it there to torture him?

- In the scene where Kramer brings day-old bagels to Jerry's apartment, George was holding a bagel when he prepared to leave. When he reached the door he turned and pointed, and was no longer holding the bagel.

Trivial Tidbits

- "The Strike" marked Bryan Cranston's final appearance as Tim Whatley on *Seinfeld*. After *Seinfeld*, he went on to even bigger and better roles.

- Around the time "The Strike" aired, it was announced that this would be the final season of *Seinfeld*.

- Tracy Letts, who played "Counterguy" at the Off-Track Betting location, successfully went on to a career as a playwright, eventually receiving the 2008 Pulitzer Prize for Drama for his play *August: Osage County*. He also received a Tony Award as an actor, for his portrayal of George in the revival of *Who's Afraid of Virginia Woolf?* We're not sure where the Pulitzer Prize is taking him, but we hear the Tony is taking him to Sardis.

- Guess who was typecast? Colin Malone, who was cast in the role as "Sleazy Guy" from the Off Track Betting location, was at the time known for his role in a Public Access TV Show called *Colin's Sleazy Friends*, a talk show about the porn industry.

- H&H Bagels is the name of a real bagel shop in New York City. The company is world famous for its bagels, and the *Seinfeld* writers regularly consumed their product.

- In the DVD commentary feature, during the scene where George receives a Festivus card from his father, Dan O'Keefe mentioned that he actually used to receive Festivus cards from his own father.

- In the scene where Frank tells Kramer about the fight for the doll, the final two lines, "That must have been some kind of doll" and "she was", were totally ad-libbed by the actors.[13]

- According to Jerry Stiller, when they were preparing for the scene where his character enters the diner with the aluminum pole, Michael Richards advised him to drag the pole along the ground.[14]   The idea was to make the hollow dragging sound, which Michael thought would make it even more hilarious. He was right!

- The idea of the "Two-Face" nickname given to the character Gwen was introduced to the episode by writer Dan O'Keefe. It was based on a woman he had met in college who often exhibited similar characteristics. O'Keefe also said that the situation always reminded him of the *Batman* character Harvey Dent, who was also nicknamed "Two-Face".[15]

- When Jerry Seinfeld and Karen Fineman (Gwen) were

shooting the scene where they were in the dark tunnel, the makeup crew put a prosthetic in Karen's mouth to puff her upper lip and tissues in her nose to flare her nostrils.[16]

- Originally, instead of using makeup gimmicks, another actress (Suzanne Krull) was cast to play "Different Gwen". It was eventually decided that using an entirely different person for the less attractive version of the character would be too confusing for the audience.[17]

- Incidentally, Gwen was Jerry's 69th successive girlfriend in the series.

- When Jerry says, "It has a certain understated stupidity" George claims he is quoting *The Outlaw Josey Wales*. Smart movie buffs will tell you that George was wrong, and the line isn't actually in the movie.

- When "Denim Vest" (Kevin McDonald) looked across the street to try to find a fake number to give Elaine, he spotted a truck labeled with the name "Azzari Brothers". This was named after *Seinfeld* set designer Tom Azzari, who is also the man shown standing in front of the truck.

- Although the episode was named "The Strike", many fans refer to this episode as "The Festivus". Even Jerry Seinfeld agrees, as he can be heard to say in the DVD commentary that if they knew what they know now, the episode would have been named "The Festivus".

- Aside from everything else this episode reveals, it also explains why Kramer never held a job throughout the show.

On the Cutting Room Floor

- Deleted from the dialogue during the scene where Jerry and Elaine were teasing George about Festivus, Jerry also asked George, "Didn't you have to sing poetry into a tape recorder and dance with your mother?"[18]

- In the original opening to the scene where Frank visits

Kramer in the bagel shop, there is a deleted portion where Kramer was shown cleaning off tables. After throwing away a plate, a customer said, "I was still eating that." In response, Kramer took the bagel out of the trash and put it back in front of the customer.[19] The customer was played by Jerry Dixon, who is credited for the episode but never shown.

- Deleted from the final dialogue in the diner was a line where Frank told Kramer he was going home to "polish the pole".[20] (Does anyone wonder why it was deleted?)

- Dropped from the scene in Jerry's apartment was a moment where Elaine dialed her blow-off number and learned it was an off-track betting "parlor". Jerry's response was, "Well, at least it's a parlor. That's kind of elegant."[21]

- Deleted from the final dialogue in the scene where Kramer sees Elaine outside the bagel shop were additional lines where he tells her she looks "lank and droopy"[22], "all scraggly like a muskrat" and "moist and squiddy".[23]

- Deleted from the final cut was a reference to the past made by the manager of the bagel shop. After not seeing Kramer for several years, he asked, "what happened to the ponytail?"[24] Kenny Kramer (the real "Kramer) would have loved this, as he actually does wear a ponytail.

- In an alternate ending to the scene where George gives Kruger a human fund card, Kruger responds, "So, you gave my gift to someone else." George's reply was, "Here, take two."[25]

- Removed from the dialogue between Gwen and Jerry in the taxi was a line where she asked Jerry what movie he wanted to see. Jerry's reply was, "Anything but Batman."[26]

- Before the Festivus dinner scene was filmed, Julia Louis Dreyfus was told that Colin Malone, the actor playing "Sleazy Guy", was a porn star. On the cutting room floor is a scene where he leans over toward Elaine and says, "I think you're a fox." Julia couldn't keep a straight face during the scene, and therefore they had to cut it out of the final episode.[27]

- Cut from the Festivus dinner scene was a line where Frank

said, "Happy Festivus Georgie. This is going to hurt you more than... I lost my train of thought."[28]

Immediate Reaction

At the time of the episode's release, writer Dan O'Keefe really had no idea how his family's zany holiday would leave a mark on society. "I was honestly surprised anyone gave a flying fuck," Dan O'Keefe told *Mother Jones* magazine in 2013.[29]

The network rating for "The Strike" was a respectable 20.2 with an audience share of 33.[30] *Seinfeld* was one of the most popular series at the time and the good ratings were not abnormal. Clearly though, the seed had been planted. As we all know, the seed grew and Festivus began to flourish.

THE FESTIVUS BUNCH

(Sung to the tune of "The Brady Bunch")

Here's the story of Dan O'Keefe
Who in the 60s created Festivus
With the airing of grievances, and feats of strength
It's for the rest of us

Here's the story of Dan's son Daniel
Who was writing for the Seinfeld TV show
He wrote Festivus into an episode
Adding an aluminum pole

Then this one day when the show was on the TV
And they saw it caused so much of a fuss
Yes it was a Festivus miracle
That's the way we all came to know Festivus
Yes Festivus, Oh Festivus
That's the way we all now know Festivus

(Parody Lyrics by Joel Kopischke)

An unadorned aluminum pole is the chief symbol of Festivus. Please note there is an electrical outlet (holes) in the lower right of this photo. However, Festivus tradition dictates there is no requirement for electrical lighting, leaving power outlets available for you to power your electric meat slicer.

Chapter 5 : The Festivus Pole

One of the oddest and most popular Festivus traditions centers around the main symbol of the holiday, the unadorned aluminum pole.

The Festivus pole was introduced to viewers as a prop in the *Seinfeld* Episode "The Strike". Frank Costanza first told Kramer about the pole when Kramer asked whether there was a "Christmas tree". Frank's quaint reply was, "No. Instead, there's a pole. Requires no decoration." Thus, the idea of a pole as a symbol was born.

The pole was strictly a *Seinfeld* creation, as the "Real Festivus" described by writer Dan O'Keefe, did not have an aluminum pole. "We embellished it a little bit with a metal pole," *Seinfeld* director Andy Ackerman has said. "If you're going to embellish with something what a great way to do it with a metal pole."[31]

As the *Seinfeld* version of Festivus originally played on television, Frank revealed his pole by dragging it into the diner and viewers were treated to a hilarious moment. They could see how it was as plain and drab as they actually imagined. Made of unpolished aluminum, it was the polar opposite of what a lush green Christmas tree is meant to represent. Unencumbered by branches and decorations, it was barren, lacked curves and was obviously not expensive.

Clearly, the aluminum pole was chosen to be the direct opposite of a commercialized, highly decorated Christmas tree. Of course, the idea that an aluminum pole should be the object of great reverence is exceptionally humorous. The comedy was enhanced by Frank stating he "finds tinsel distracting" and praising the aluminum pole for its "very high strength-to-weight ratio."

One other important Festivus fact gleaned by watching the *Seinfeld* episode is how Frank stores his aluminum pole in the "crawlspace". This is exactly why Festivus fans worldwide make a special note to store their poles in out of the way places such as attics, basements, closets or (yes) even a crawlspace.

It should be noted that the pole used in "The Strike" did actually come from something akin to a crawlspace. According to Mike Burns, who worked as a grip on the Seinfeld set, Frank's Festivus pole was an 8 foot tall, 1.5 inch interior diameter, "Schedule 80" aluminum "speed rail" that came from a storage location under the audience bleachers. In set jargon, a speed rail is a multi-purpose "erector set" used for lighting rigs, camera mounts, handrails, etc. In the scene where the pole was erected at the Costanza residence, it was attached to the floor inside a rounded speed rail foot flange which was screwed to the floor with drywall screws and fender washers. Mike is happy to say that he was the one to secure the pole to the base and tighten the set screw that day. "Being the erector of the Festivus pole was one of my iconic Seinfeld moments, and one with vast implications. It was an impressive feat of strength, you might say," Mike proudly adds.

How to get a Festivus Pole?

There are places on the web where you may order a pole, such as FestivusPoles.com. The website is run by a legitimate company, The Wagner Companies, a Milwaukee based metal manufacturer who has been in business since 1850. They produce an excellent product. There is more about The Wagner Companies later in this chapter.

Now, do you think that Frank Costanza ordered his pole from a web site? To a "Costanza", Festivus poles don't come from a commercial enterprise. However, they might be scavenged from a work site, a vacant lot around the corner, or stripped from a pole lamp found at the local thrift store.

Poles come from the crawlspace, and not from the mailman! If

You can find plenty of metal poles down at the hardware store. Just make sure it's aluminum (not steel), and ask the clerk to cut it down to size.

you desire an authentic Festivus experience, take this into consideration. Besides, who can trust a mailman?

You can also buy an aluminum pole from the local hardware store. You might find that they sell aluminum poles in ten or twelve foot lengths. Make sure you get aluminum and not steel. Outside the strength-to-weight ratio, the difference is negligible; however, it would be akin to hauling a birch tree into the house for Christmas. Not cool! Consider asking someone at the hardware store to cut the pole down to a more functional length.

After you get it home, you can fashion a stand in your workshop, or use an old Christmas tree stand. Another popular method of erecting your pole (*that's what she said*) is to anchor it in a large flowerpot or planter filled with sand or gravel. An engineer would tell you that you need to have a good anchor, as the moment of force caused by the length of the upright pole... blah blah blah. I'm not an engineer, but I'll just say, make sure you have a good base!

The best advice for a novice Festivus celebrant is to keep it simple. Head to your crawlspace (or attic, basement or closet) and find out what you do have. Do you have an old lamp pole or curtain rod? Maybe a wooden plank or a cardboard tube you could cover in aluminum foil. Anything that is non-commercial and non-flashy. This is the true spirit of Festivus.

If you are determined to have an actual aluminum pole then go to the junkyard and find one. If that fails, then buy one online or go to the hardware store and buy a cheap piece of aluminum tube. Make sure that you are rude to the salesperson and try to barter the price down, because that's what Frank Costanza would have done.

Do "Festivus Poles" come from Wisconsin?

Tony Leto, Executive Vice President, Sales and Marketing of The Wagner Companies in Milwaukee is a *Seinfeld* fan. In fact, he grew up in New York and actually went to Queens College with Jerry Seinfeld, where they both were theatre/television majors.

"He graduated in '76 and I graduated in '75," Tony explained. "I remained aware of him after college as his comedy career started to take off, started watching the show once it first aired and remain a fan to this day."

In December 2004, after an article exposing the popularity of Festivus appeared in the New York Times, Tony had a notion. Why not manufacture and sell Festivus poles?

"That article touched on how seven years after Festivus was introduced on *Seinfeld*, it was actually being celebrated," Tony said. "As I was reading the article, I particularly noted that the centerpiece of Festivus was an aluminum pole. Once I returned to the office after the New Year, I mentioned this article to Bob Wagner (the owner of The Wagner Companies)." Tony suggested that they could easily turn their stock of aluminum pipe into Festivus poles, and while they both knew it likely would not turn

Festivus poles are packaged at the Wagner Companies in Milwaukee, Wisconsin.

into major profits for the company, they figured they might get some press and have some fun.

Soon they had reserved the domain festivuspoles.com, and a website was built. By the time Festivus 2005 had arrived, they had developed their pole, along with a unique collapsible base, and had inventory on-hand for sale.

"That first year we sold about 200, but did get some good press coverage and had fun -- as we had hoped," Tony said.

The next year, after they received additional press coverage, sales peaked at approximately 700 poles. Then in 2007, for a marketing stunt, they opened the world's first Festivus pole lot in downtown Milwaukee. It was held in conjunction with the Brady Street Festivus celebration, a yearly Milwaukee tradition. "Unfortunately, there was a large snow storm and it was extremely cold," Tony said. "While some people did make a point of coming by, it was just too cold for us to consider doing it again. We have had people who have wanted to do their own Festivus pole lot, but to date no one else has ever taken the task on. As you are well aware, extreme cold and metal poles do not play well together."

Today, The Wagner Companies remains the world's largest manufacturer and supplier of aluminum Festivus poles. How do they feel when they are referred to as the source of the "official" Festivus pole, as some people have unilaterally decided?

"We're proud to be known as the official Festivus pole," Tony said. "We were the first to market, and we registered the trademark for 'Festivus poles' so no one else can sell a product and call it a 'Festivus Pole'. We were able to get the trademark as the term 'Festivus Pole' was not used in the Festivus episode -- it was only referred to as an 'aluminum pole'."

Tony went on to explain that they have arranged for another company to license the "Festivus Pole" trademark so they may offer a Festivus pole, which is packaged with the *Seinfeld* brand. "However," Tony clarifies, "they produce theirs in stainless steel and only offer a desktop size."

Tony added a little perspective, "If you consider that we are in the business of selling metal, we have sold about 12 tons of aluminum pipe in the form of Festivus poles over the last 10 years."

We know that Frank Costanza chose an aluminum pole for its high strength-to-weight ratio. Tony likes to joke, "Milwaukee is also known for its high strength-to-weight ratio."

However, with all the connections between Wisconsin and Festivus, is Wisconsin the center of the Festivus universe? "It's likely that the fact Festivus poles are produced in Wisconsin may be what has put the state at the center of the Festivus universe, but we also had a former governor, Jim Doyle, who was known to quote *Seinfeld* in the state house and posed proudly with his Festivus pole back in 2005," Tony adds. "Milwaukee is also the home of Joel Kopischke who has written two great Festivus songs."

Maybe there is something to this?

Incidentally, Governor Doyle's Festivus pole is now part of the collection at the Wisconsin State Historical Society. If that doesn't cement Wisconsin as the center of the Festivus universe, we don't know what does.

a broom shaft
painted silver
pared back elegance
shoddy wooden makeshift base
spray painted to appear aluminum

not so shiny duct tape

tinsel can be distracting
antique silver art deco lamp
fence railing
walking stick very simple

covered in aluminium foil
small pole broken shovel handle

high strength to weight ratio

Aluminum pole
Bamboo pole covered in foil

Unadorned round piece of wood
Part of a pool skimmer pole Festivuspoles.com

without decoration
light saber tent pole keep it in the garage
wrapping paper tubes

Plastic plumbing pipe
painted glossy silver
conduit

Festivus Pole
silver Dr. Pepper cans
old rusty tree holder straight up aluminum
six feet tall
aluminum
strong aircraft grade Aluminum tubing
extension pole bare pole with stand
Shower curtain rod
whatever is handy slender
5 ft
Just a pole! found in a junk pile
No adornments Coors Light cans
christmas tree holder
Plain Festivus
We posted our grievances on the pole
flagpole
old broom stripper pole

A word cloud of terms people used when asked the question
"describe your pole".

49

What do other People Use?

Other than an actual aluminum pole bought online or at the hardware store, what are some of the other items that people use as a Festivus pole?

When we asked the visitors to FestivusWeb.com to "describe their pole" this is some of the feedback we received (Sorry, we didn't include the dirty responses):

- An old shower curtain rod.
- A PVC pipe in a Christmas tree holder, then painted glossy silver.
- 5 feet of Coors Light cans.
- Soda pop cans stacked upon each other and then fastened together with duct tape.
- An old broom.
- A bamboo pole covered in foil.
- A lamp, without the shade.
- Plastic plumbing pipe painted with silver acrylic paint.
- A bird feeder extension pole.
- Part of a pool skimmer.
- A broken shovel handle, covered in duct tape and held in an old rusty Christmas tree stand.
- A flagpole bought on clearance.
- A light saber.
- A window curtain rod.
- Old wrapping paper rolls covered in aluminum foil.
- A broom shaft, spray painted to appear aluminum.
- A walking stick.
- A fence railing mounted on two boards nailed together.
- An aluminum tent pole.

TIP! If you decide to use the curtain rod from the front window as your Festivus pole, make sure you don't walk around nude until Festivus has ended. There are stringent laws in most places!

How to Decorate a Festivus Pole

How do you decorate a Festivus pole? You don't! In the spirit of Frank Costanza, who had a completely bare and unadorned pole, do not decorate your Festivus pole. Frank remarked that tinsel was distracting, which was his reason for not decorating the pole. Most people respect Frank's wishes and leave their Festivus pole unencumbered by any decorative device.

You may need to label your pole, especially if you are displaying it outdoors where passersby and your neighbors may see it. You might place a sign atop the pole, or next to the pole that says, "Happy Festivus" or "A Festivus for the Rest of Us". This should suffice in getting your message across. After all, you don't want your neighbors and other slack-jawed yokels knocking on your door and asking you about the strange pole in your yard.

However, when it comes to Festivus, we don't make the rules. You make the rules. It is important to admit that this is one of the cornerstones of Festivus! It is the holiday for the rest of us, and if you want to put lights, balls and garland on your Festivus pole, just go right ahead. You can even put tinsel on it if you so desire, just remember that you're liable to give Frank Costanza a heart attack.

Keep in mind, if you wish to celebrate a completely traditional Frank Costanza style Festivus, then keep your aluminum pole unadorned and tinsel free. It's your choice.

Festivus Pole Care

Here are some basic tips for the care of your Festivus pole...

You don't really need to do anything to the pole. Just bring it out at Festivus time, and display it. When Festivus is over put the pole away in a safe place like a crawlspace, attic, garage or shed.

Don't polish it, even if it looks dingy. It's supposed to look that way! It needs to retain its dull finish. However, if the pole has a natural sheen, don't worry about reducing its luster. That's too much work. It's always good enough as it is. Mind you, if the dog pees on it, then you should probably wash it. Just take it out back and hose it down. Problem solved!

Festivus Pole Safety Tips

Here are some safety tips for the use of your Festivus pole:

- Don't let any guests climb the pole. They could hurt the pole.
- A Festivus pole is not a "Dancing" pole. Pole dancing should only be attempted by professionals.
- During the Feats of Strength, don't let anyone joust with the Festivus pole. Just send them back to the renaissance fair they came from.
- If the pole is outdoors in below zero temperatures, don't let anyone lick the pole. It's tempting, as the pole can be sexy when it's frosty, but don't let them do it!

A dancing pole could double as a Festivus pole, but a Festivus pole is never a dancing pole.

Beer Can Festivus Poles

You can make a reasonable facsimile of a Festivus pole out of aluminum beer cans. It's been done a few times and even by a certain atheist who just loves to torture Christians in Florida.

How is it done?

Method 1 (For fancy people):
1. Buy a twenty-four pack of canned beer.
2. Drink all the beer. Rinse out the cans as you drink them.
3. **Sober up.** *(Make sure to do this before proceeding to Step 4!)*

4. Using a band saw cut off the top and the bottom of each beer can.

5. Build a base out of wood (crossed boards) and glue a vertical PVC pipe on the base. The PVC pipe needs to be just smaller than the diameter of the beer cans.

6. Slide the beer cans onto the PVC pipe until it is completely covered by the aluminum sheath of beer cans.

7. Keep the top on the top-most can.

8. When you are done, you should have a perfectly straight and sturdy beer can Festivus pole.

Method 2 (The hillbilly method):

1. Buy a twenty-four pack of canned beer.

2. Find a flat piece of wood, at least two feet square. This is your base.

3. After you drink the first beer, hot glue the can vertically to the center of the board.

4. Leave the board in your workshop. As you drink each of the beers, over the next few days, keep hot-gluing each can to the top of the previous can.

5. When you have finished the beer you will have a tall, crooked, smelly beer can Festivus pole.

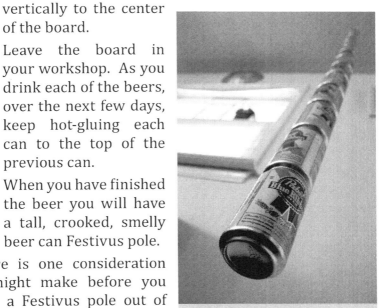

A beer can Festivus pole made from a stack of Pabst Blue Ribbon... burrrlappp!

There is one consideration you might make before you create a Festivus pole out of beer cans: Your pole is now decorated by the brand of beer that you bought. It's not really

An old Christmas tree stand works well as a Festivus pole base.

a plain and unadorned aluminum pole. This may be unsatisfactory to some folks, however, when you consider that you are not spending much money on the pole and that you are doing something which in essence is pretty funny, the spirit of Festivus is still there. Plus, you are enjoying a bunch of beer and supporting the struggling beer industry. A team of Clydesdales doesn't come cheap, you know. Mind you, this could all be done with soda cans. But, where is the fun in that?

The Festivus Pole Base

Many people have manufactured homemade Festivus poles and stood them up in old Christmas tree stands, flowerpots or planters filled with sand or rocks, or attached them to a home-made wooden base. You can also go baseless and just lean your pole up against the wall, or lash it to a piece of furniture such as a table leg or to the decorative cornice on your antique armoire.

Festivus Pole Etiquette

If you walk anywhere with your Festivus pole, you should drag it on the ground, just as Frank Costanza did when he entered the diner. It made a wonderful hollow sound as it resonated on the tiled floor. That's the sound of Festivus! You should also wear a trench coat and gloves as well. Not because you wish to be exactly like Frank Costanza, more so because it's usually cold at Festivus time.

When somebody introduces you to their Festivus pole you should reply politely with words such as, "I find your belief system fascinating". It may also be appropriate to make a statement related to the strength-to-weight ratio of the pole such as, "What's the strength-to-weight ratio of that baby?"

Demonstrating genuine interest in another's Festivus pole is good manners. You might also comment how the pole is "straight" and "tall", or you may describe a Festivus pole as "beautiful", or more simply as a "beauty". If you do it correctly, you may see the pole owner blush.

It's also polite to refer to it as a "good pole" or a "worthy pole", though you should never call it "poleworthy".

It's only good Festivus etiquette to follow these guidelines.

"Meh" adorns the Festivus pole by Chrissy and Danny. It's easy! Just stab your pole in a bucket of quick drying cement and say, "Meh."

Make sure you serve your meatloaf on a bed of lettuce, a la
Estelle Costanza. It's important!

Chapter 6 : Festivus Dinner

A formal family dinner is the customary focal point for Festivus. Dinner is featured in both the O'Keefe and *Seinfeld* versions of the holiday, and serves as the beginning point of the celebration. The dinner allows the celebrants to gather together and focus on the holiday at hand.

What are some of the traditions of Festivus Dinner? Currently, the traditions people follow are derived from what was seen in the Costanza Festivus on *Seinfeld* and from the tradition of the real Festivus, as celebrated by the O'Keefe family. Let us review these traditions.

The O'Keefe Festivus Dinner

The O'Keefe's Festivus took on the look and feel of a special family dinner. Turkey, ham or lamb chops would be served as well as all the fixings. There would be Play-Doh at the place settings and the diners would be encouraged to sculpt something creative. The adults would drink champagne. For dessert, there would be a Pepperidge Farm cake, usually decorated with M&Ms.

The Costanza Festivus Dinner

In the *Seinfeld* episode "The Strike," a celebratory dinner is shown on the evening of Festivus. The meal appeared to be meat loaf on a bed of lettuce (once thought to be spaghetti). The only other item on the table appeared to be a bowl of peas. The table was set formally. No alcohol was served, however George Costanza's boss, Mr. Kruger, drank from a flask he pulled from his inside jacket pocket.

The Official Festivus Dish - Meatloaf

Many people like to stay true to the traditional *Seinfeld* Festivus, and they serve meatloaf at their Festivus Dinner.

What about spaghetti? Wasn't spaghetti once considered as a candidate for Festivus Dinner? If you thought so you are correct. It was! However, things have evolved.

Since "The Strike" was aired in 1997, the traditional meal for Festivus immediately became known as "Spaghetti or Meatloaf". The choice was due to the fact nobody could actually identify the meal. Estelle Costanza was observed serving a reddish food on top of a whitish base. In fact, it rather looked like red spaghetti sauce on a bed of noodles. Still, some folks thought the dish look sliced, like meatloaf. However, they had reservations about the light-colored foodstuff that was shown under the meatloaf. It just wasn't clear.

Now, fast forward to more modern times. With the advent of larger television screens (including HDTV), it is clearly seen to be slices of meatloaf on a bed of lettuce. Although, the notion of serving meatloaf on lettuce still seems odd to some people, we have to remember that this is an odd family celebrating an odd holiday. So, it just seems to be perfectly acceptable.

In 2013, FestivusWeb.com began an online poll to see how website visitors identified the meal. 82% of the respondents thought it was meatloaf, 8% said it was spaghetti and 10% voted that it was "something else" (clearly the jackass vote).

We all know that website polls are exceedingly scientific. This makes it official! The masses have spoken and the ruling is that Estelle Costanza served meatloaf.

What do other people serve at Festivus?

Aside from the meatloaf option, are you still wondering what you should be serving at your Festivus gathering? It seems that most people go with dishes that have been featured in *Seinfeld*.

Some of these foods have now attained a cult-like status. Last

If someone brings a Marble Rye, don't forget to put it out!

December in a local bakery I asked for a loaf of marble rye. After the clerk fetched the bread I asked if they had any black and white cookies, to which the clerk replied, "Are you Seinfeld?" I laughed it off, but took note of the evidence toward the lasting impact of *Seinfeld* in popular culture.

Certainly, this is why people serve foods like Junior Mints and chocolate babka at Festivus. It's because people love to be reminded of *Seinfeld*. Don't forget, the whole point is to make your Festivus celebration fun and memorable!

Are you still pondering what to serve? We have a comprehensive compendium of *Seinfeld* Foods in Appendix A. We have also included a few recipes in the next few pages. Remember, you are the chef. You decide. There is plenty from which to choose!

Festivus Recipes

We have included some special recipes for Festivus favorites. You can probably find similar recipes online, or in Grandma's old cookbook, but trust me... these are better.

Happy Festivus Meatloaf

There's nuttin' finer than a big slab of meatloaf on Festivus. This recipe serves eight... six if you slice it thick.

Ingredients
- 2 eggs
- 2/3 cup milk
- 1/4 tsp ground pepper
- 2 tsp salt
- 3 slices of fresh bread, crumbled
- 1 finely chopped medium-sized onion
- 1 clove of garlic, very finely chopped
- 1-1/2 lbs lean ground beef
- 1/4 cup brown sugar
- 1/4 cup ketchup
- 1 tbsp prepared mustard

Preparation
1. Beat eggs lightly with fork.
2. Add the milk, salt, pepper and bread crumbs, then beat the mixture until the bread disintegrates.
3. Add the onions, garlic and the ground beef, mixing well with your hands.
4. Once it's mixed thoroughly, pack the meat mixture into a baking pan. A bread loaf pan is perfect.
5. Combine the brown sugar, ketchup and mustard and spread all over the loaf.
6. Bake in a 350 degree oven for 1 hr. Let stand 15 minutes, and then remove from pan.
7. Slice into fat chunks. Serve on a bed of lettuce (Estelle Costanza style).
8. Some folks may also like additional ketchup on the side, or even salsa. But, not seltzer.

A steaming hot bowl of Mulligatawny soup goes well with Junior Mints, Ovaltine and *Seinfeld* Season 9.

Kramer Style Mulligatawny

This makes a large pot of Mulligatawny and will serve 6-8 large Kramer-sized bowls. Good enough for a Festivus Party, or at any time of the year that you need something hot and tasty. The best part of this soup is that you can get Kramer to watch over your armoire if you promise him a bowlful.

Tip: To make this dish truly "Kramer Style" make sure you get free ingredients from your neighbor.

Ingredients
- 2-3 boneless chicken breasts or thighs, cooked and diced
- 1 cup cooked white or brown rice
- 1 medium sized yellow/white onion, diced
- 4 to 6 carrots, diced
- 4 celery stalks, diced
- 1/2 cup butter

- 8 cups chicken stock
- 3 heaping tablespoons all-purpose flour
- 5 rounded teaspoons Curry Powder
- 2 apples, peeled, cored and diced
- 1 teaspoon salt
- 1/4 teaspoon dried thyme
- 1/2 teaspoon pepper
- 1 cup milk

Ensure you have all the ingredients! Of course, check your neighbors' pantry in advance. If they don't have a certain ingredient, make sure you place the item on their shopping list.

Directions

1. Prepare your chicken. Slice 2-3 boneless chicken breasts or boneless thighs into strips and sauté in a pan. Cook thoroughly but don't overcook. Remove from the pan and let cool, then dice into bite-sized chunks. Place aside.
2. Prepare one cup of white or brown rice. Place aside.
3. Dice onion, carrots and celery stalks.
4. In a stockpot, place the vegetables, butter and 2 cups of chicken stock. Bring to a boil and simmer until vegetables are tender.
5. Stir in flour and curry powder and boil gently for three more minutes until thickened slightly.
6. Add the remaining chicken stock and reduce to a simmer for 30 minutes.
7. Add chicken, salt, pepper, thyme, rice and diced apple. Simmer for another 30 minutes.
8. Add 1 cup of milk, stir and simmer on low for 15 minutes.
9. Serve. Watch the knees buckle.

Nothing could be more Seinfeldian than a batch of black and white cookies.

"Look to the Cookie" Black and White Cookies

These cake-style cookies are a staple in New York City bakeries. They are guaranteed to make you feel good all over, and certainly won't spoil your non-vomit streak. Makes two-dozen cookies.

Ingredients:
- **Cookies:**
  - 1 cup unsalted butter
  - 1 3/4 cups white sugar
  - 4 eggs
  - 1 cup milk
  - 1/2 teaspoon vanilla extract
  - 1/4 teaspoon lemon extract
  - 2 1/2 cups cake flour
  - 2 1/2 cups all-purpose flour
  - 1 teaspoon baking powder
  - 1/2 teaspoon salt
- **Icing:**
  - 4 cups confectioners' sugar
  - 1/3 cup boiling water

- 1 (1 ounce) square bittersweet chocolate, chopped

Directions

1. Preheat oven to 375 degrees Fahrenheit.
2. In a medium bowl cream butter and sugar.
3. Beat in eggs one at a time, add milk, vanilla, lemon extract and mix.
4. Combine the cake flour and all-purpose flour, baking powder, and salt. Stir into egg mixture until well blended.
5. Grease 2 cookie sheets.
6. Drop round, tablespoon-sized balls of dough 2 inches apart on cookie sheets.
7. Bake at 375 F until edges just begin to brown, about 20 to 30 minutes. The balls of dough should have melted down into flat, round cookies.
8. Transfer to racks and cool completely.
9. While cookies are still baking, place the confectioners' sugar in a large bowl. Mix in boiling water one tablespoon at a time until mixture is thick and spreadable.
10. Put chopped chocolate in a microwave-safe bowl and heat at 50% power for 1 minute; remove and stir. Continue heating in 30 second intervals. Stir after each interval until melted, then stir the melted chocolate into half of the icing and let cool.
11. With two separate pastry brushes, coat half of each cookie with chocolate icing and the other half with white icing. The icing should be placed on the bottom (flat side) of the cookie.
12. Set on waxed paper until icing hardens. (30 minutes)
13. Serve! Make sure you say "look to the cookie" as you take a huge bite.

Costanza Style Paella

Perfect for when you invite Morty and Helen Seinfeld over for dinner. This recipe makes eight servings... just the right amount. You don't want to make too much! After all, if the guests don't show, who's going to eat all the paella?

Ingredients
- 2 tablespoons olive oil
- 1 tablespoon paprika
- 2 teaspoons dried oregano
- Salt and black pepper to taste
- 2 pounds skinless, boneless chicken breasts, cut into 2 inch pieces
- 2 tablespoons olive oil
- 3 cloves garlic, crushed
- 1 teaspoon crushed red pepper flakes
- 2 cups uncooked short-grain white rice
- 1 pinch saffron threads
- 1 bay leaf
- 1/2 bunch parsley, chopped
- 1 quart chicken stock
- 2 lemons, zested
- 2 tablespoons olive oil
- 1 Spanish onion, chopped
- 1 red bell pepper, coarsely chopped
- 1 pound chorizo sausage, casings removed and crumbled
- 1 pound shrimp, peeled and deveined

Directions
1. In a medium bowl, mix together olive oil, paprika, oregano, and salt and pepper. Stir in chicken pieces to coat. Cover, and refrigerate for a few hours.
2. Heat 2 tablespoons olive oil in a large skillet or paella

pan over medium heat. Stir in garlic, red pepper flakes, and rice. Cook, stirring, to coat rice with oil, about 3 minutes. Stir in saffron threads, bay leaf, parsley, chicken stock, and lemon zest. Bring to a boil, cover, and reduce heat to medium low. Simmer 20 minutes.

3.   Meanwhile, heat 2 tablespoons of olive oil in a separate skillet over medium heat. Stir in marinated chicken and onion; cook 5 minutes. Stir in bell pepper and sausage; cook 5 minutes. Stir in shrimp; cook, turning the shrimp, until both sides are pink.

4.   Spread rice mixture onto a serving tray. Top with meat and seafood mixture.

5.   Serve. Hopefully you haven't made too much!

Chapter 7 : The Airing of Grievances

According to the *Seinfeld* character Frank Costanza, the celebration of Festivus doesn't officially start until the Airing of Grievances begins, which takes place immediately after the Festivus dinner has been served.

> **Frank Costanza:** *Welcome, newcomers. The tradition of Festivus begins with the Airing of Grievances.*

Of course, the Airing of Grievances we refer to was invented by the character Frank Costanza and demonstrated in the *Seinfeld* episode "The Strike", where the purpose was clearly defined:

> **Frank Costanza:** *You gather your family around, and tell them all the ways they have disappointed you over the past year!*

People normally complain when their dissatisfaction reaches some sort of critical threshold. Telling others of your complaints is seen as a possible means to reduce the problem, and it can serve as a cathartic method to cleanse people of the evils of dissatisfaction. With Festivus you are encouraged to complain in the Airing of Grievances, essentially ferreting out your bad feelings in an orgasm of griping.

Frank is correct in his assertion that you should air grievances with your family. After all, who is more worthy of your gripes than those you are closest to? However, we immediately notice when Frank does actually air a grievance, he doesn't direct it towards family. Instead, he complains about a visitor to the party, George's boss, Mr. Kruger. Also, in looking back at the episode, it seems that it is only the head of the family that has the privilege of airing grievances, as only Frank does so. However, in practice, it is more than common for all participants to actively air their grievances at Festivus.

It should also be noted, in the O'Keefe family Festivus there was a specific time where all family members were called upon to tell what irked them. While it was not actually labeled as "Airing of Grievances", the O'Keefe tradition was the actual source for the *Seinfeld* version of the ritual.

Tips for the Airing of Grievances

In the Costanza household, Festivus is the time of the year to tell friends and family about how they disappointed you in the past year. This can be fun and dangerous. Who doesn't love complaining? In contrast, who actually loves being complained about? You should seriously consider that it is probably not the time or place to get too personal. Here are some additional tips you might consider for your Airing of Grievances.

- If your group is shy and not willing to air their grievances publicly, a useful recommendation is to anonymously write grievances on sticky notes and post them to the Festivus pole. In fact, this has become one of the most popular methods for many folks who celebrate Festivus. Sometimes the grievances are later read aloud, or they are simply left on the pole for all to admire casually.

- If you like, you can put everyone's grievances in a hat or a bag (stuff your sorries in a sack, Mister!) and read them out anonymously. In this case, the "grievor" remains a mystery, but the "grievee" is still on the hook for the complaint. This may not be an optimal scenario if you are surrounded by despicable people who may enjoy the opportunity for a drive-by character assassination.

- If your family and friends are more reserved, keep the airing of grievances portion of the celebration short, or possibly include a rule that the only personal grievances that may

Keep a miniature Festivus pole nearby. Stick your grievances to the pole as they arise. When Festivus arrives... you are ready to complain!

be aired must be directed to those who did not attend the gathering, especially those that were invited but chose not to come (fair game). Public figures such as politicians and celebrities are always fair game.

- Include newcomers! Just like Frank Costanza who begins his Airing of Grievances by taking on George's boss Mr. Kruger, don't forget to include guests (newcomers) to your list of people that you may have grievances about.

    Frank Costanza: *You, Kruger. My son tells me your company stinks! You couldn't smooth a silk sheet if you had a hot date with a babe...I lost my train of thought.*

- Don't lose your train of thought! Don't end up in the same situation as Frank. If you have to, write your grievances on a slip of paper or note cards beforehand, just in case your train of thought is easily derailed.

How do others handle the Airing of Grievances?

Airing of Grievances can be tricky business. How can you possibly hold a successful airing of grievances and still maintain harmony between your friends and family? Let's have a look at how others do it.

In 2014, FestivusWeb.com asked its visitors to complete a survey detailing how they air their grievances. It was discovered that 87% of respondents said that they actually do participate in an Airing of Grievances at Festivus-time. Of course, this means that 13% of respondents said that they never do any complaining at Festivus. Interesting!

In addition, we asked those respondents who indicated that they participate in the Airing of Grievances to give us more details as to what they actually do:

- 61% tell others how they've disappointed them in the past year.
- 20% write their grievances on notes and stick them to the Festivus pole.
- 19% usually keep their grievances to themselves.

We also asked people to specifically "Describe their Airing of Grievances tradition". The feedback we received is interesting and useful:

- Grievances have to be either haiku or iambic pentameter.
- We "aye" or "nay" each grievance and argue about the worthiness and validity of the complaint.
- Grievances are light-hearted followed by a gag gift after each grievance.
- We hand out lemons with grievances and then take the lemons the next day and make lemonade. "When life hands you lemons, make lemonade!"
- We air our grievances against our pets too.
- We just whine about the government.
- There was a lot of wine to accompany the whine of recitation.

- Grievances are aired not just towards the guests, but towards anybody who has disappointed or wronged you.
- We choose someone to take them off the pole and read them and try to guess who wrote it and who it is meant for. All names are left off. Turns out to be a really funny event.
- We turn all the grievances against anyone in the room into a compliment.
- After they've been aired, the grievances are thrown into the fire, never to be mentioned again.
- A healthy amount of alcohol is served to dull the personalization of the insults.
- It's done during dinner, usually one at a time, going around the table.
- We write grievances on glass ornaments and save them from year to year. We have a bucket of them now.
- It's mostly tongue-in-cheek stuff. We're all friends, after all. It's more like a celebrity roast than a Frank Costanza shouting session.
- We all grieve together... loudly speaking over one another.
- People write their grievances and place them in a shoe box. We read them aloud at the end of the night.
- We read them aloud, and then vote on the best grievances and award prizes.
- We all sit around and tell each other we have a lot of problems with each other!
- We drink a cocktail after each one is stated.
- All guests are encouraged to show as much emotion as possible and to all talk at the same time. Swearing, finger pointing, name calling and crying are all considered appropriate behavior.
- No, we just say how we "Have a lot of problems with you people". Not only is it in *Seinfeld*, but it's also my

mother's saying which she says at other times of the year besides the holidays.

- Grievances are usually light-hearted. When someone gets a grievance sent in their direction, they are supposed to respond with "Serenity Now!"

The most commonly heard response is how people mostly joke about the grievances, and do not actually air anything specific. For some people, this keeps the family unit in harmony. After all, we can't all be Costanzas. If this method keeps your family happy then it is probably for the best.

What are some of the Best Grievances?

These are some of the best grievances we have received in the past year. If you don't have anything to complain about, you'll surely find something on this list to which you can relate...

Work Related Gripes...
- Corporate-speak. "Reach out to" (a client) sounds like a cult.
- I do not need to be best buds with the people I work with.
- Why the hell am I at work on Festivus?
- Not receiving my Christmas bonus! Sucks big time. Managers got theirs.
- I am sick of the woman in the cube next to me coming in when she should be on PTO (Paid Time Off). I cannot play "Pandora" at loud volumes when she is here.
- I'm sick of being micro-managed at work. I'm a responsible adult, I know how to do my job!
- My coworkers have B.O. and I wish they would all take a shower. I gave them soap.
- My clients are constantly trying to chisel me.
- The use of the word "OVERSIGHT". What does it mean? They used to say, "I'm sorry, that was an OVERSIGHT." Now they say programs require MORE OVERSIGHT. Does that mean they will be more ignorant of it?

The great grievance ape has a lot of problems with you people!

- Co-workers who think its okay to cut their fingernails at work while everyone else is working.
- I do not like the smell of your coffee breath. Please back off, close talker!
- I can't stand the use of "team" anymore in the workplace ... "my 'team' is working on that report" ... "the commercial 'team' is doing a great job this year" ... "the product development 'team' is handling that situation." I may work with you, but if we we're on a "team", to me that means softball, or bowling, or something like that.
- I have problems with people who sing while they're working. Do you really think that I come to my office every day to listen to your off-key tunes?
- To the guy at work who spends 75% of his day in the crapper, enough!

If life actually was an episode of Seinfeld...

- They can TAKE the reservations, but they can't KEEP the reservations.

- What the hell is that supposed to mean? You want a piece of me?
- I find tinsel distracting.
- People who have ponies! They're the worst!
- The fact that there is fat in non-fat frozen yogurt.
- Who said that nutcase Lloyd Braun could sell more computers than me!
- My iron couldn't smooth a silk sheet if it had a hot date with a babe... I lost my train of thought.

If only everyone else could drive...
- Slow drivers in the left lane!
- GOGO drivers! grrrr (gas on, gas off, gas on, gas off)! Get outta the way already!
- Tailgaters! How can you drive glued to my bumper? How does my butt smell?

Social networking complaints...
- People, who aren't dining alone, immersed in their cell phones at restaurants.
- I object to all the people who've almost collided with me while they stare down at their texts.
- People who invite me to play Facebook games.
- People who boast how wonderful their lives are on Facebook, when I know they are miserable.
- People who tweet. Nobody really cares what the hell you're doing.

Fashion faux pas...
- Hipsters in their sweaters and beard ornaments taking over my city!
- People who wear pajamas and slippers in public; seriously how hard is it to put on some clothes!
- Sweats with elastic on the bottom rarely exist anymore.

Politics...

- Generally, politicians of all political colors and stripes "suck".
- Just about everyone in the government and all bureaucrats everywhere.

Sports

- The Bears! What an embarrassment.

The never-ending whines of the Grammar Nazis...

- People who don't know the difference between "your" and "you're".
- It's not it's. It's its.
- My mother makes me take out the trash when I text and misspell.

People! They're the worst...

- Can we do something about people who smack their gum and pop it really loud?
- If anyone calls you a turkey be insulted, very insulted. Turkeys are the dumbest animals.
- I'm exhausted by passive aggressive people!
- Customers who don't know the year, make and model of the vehicle they own.
- Self-involved people, who don't know the definition of conversation...
- Why use the phrase, "I'm just saying?" What else are you doing?
- People who don't return their shopping cart to the cart corral and leave it in the middle of the parking lot to roll into someone else's car.

Everything else...

- I can decide for MYSELF how many Dr. Peppers to drink per day!
- My teenage child cannot stand that we have no "food" in

the house, only "ingredients".

- People who actually think wishing "Happy Holidays" or "Season's Greetings" is a war on Christmas!
- People talking to you about *Frozen* or *Game of Thrones* like you actually care.
- I can't stand that smug look on Tom Hanks' face. That guy is the worst.
- My five-year-old granddaughter made sure we had the Festivus pole up! Her grievance – her two year old brother ate her cookies!
- Bacon and beer are so expensive.
- Neighbors that park their car in the street and leave their driveways empty!!!
- Telemarketers and scam artists can stop calling all hours of the day and night. If any police or government service can stop these people, then what are they waiting for?
- Service people who say, "there ya go."
- My friends made fun of my damn meatloaf.
- Why can't I be given the chance to debunk the whole "winning the lottery ruined my life" myth?
- Gluten free food? How about maybe I want to eat gluten!
- Parents who enter their children in cutest kid contests and they know damn good and well their kids look like Woody Allen!
- I don't like whiners... Oh wait.

One Last Grievance...

Former *Seinfeld* writer Dan O'Keefe volunteered his own grievance at the conclusion of a *CNN* interview he gave in 2013, striking out at a known political figure: "When Rand Paul tries to seem relevant with 15-year-old pop cultural references, it reminds me of when Bob Hope used to dress up like the Fonz."[32]

Ba-da-bing!

Chapter 8 : The Feats of Strength

Normally conducted immediately following the Festivus dinner, the Feats of Strength is the final tradition observed in Festivus. *Seinfeld* folklore implies that the Feats of Strength is a competition that takes the form of a son attempting to best his father (the head of the household) in a wrestling match. However, this is not the only prescribed method, as the *Seinfeld* episode implies that a guest may also wrestle the head of the house.

Who doesn't love a good, old-fashioned wrestling match? Antique furniture collectors might possibly take umbrage to people tossing their sweaty bodies around the living room.

Classic greek wrestling as depicted in statue form. Do you think Frank and George Costanza stripped naked before they engaged in manly combat?

They should probably consider dragging their antique armoire out onto the sidewalk while Festivus takes its ultimate course. Better yet, they could participate in a low impact competition; an alternative that the entire gathering might enjoy. We have several alternative activity suggestions later in this chapter.

Interestingly, Feats of Strength weren't part of the real Festivus, practiced by the O'Keefe family. "I was not forced to wrestle my father," Dan O'Keefe has said. "If I had, I would've been raised by the state of New York."[33]

The Seinfeld Feats of Strength

As depicted in *Seinfeld*, the Feats of Strength normally follow the Airing of Grievances. Curiously though, in *Seinfeld* the actual Feats of Strength are never shown. In the episode, Frank Costanza clearly states, "Until you pin me, George, Festivus is not over!" This leaves us no choice but to imagine the pending outcome. It should also be noted that the notion Festivus ends when the "head of the household" is pinned is an extrapolation of what is actually portrayed in *Seinfeld*, as the expression "head of the household" is never actually uttered in the episode.

In the episode, we can clearly see that George did not appreciate the Feats of Strength. This was evident when Frank played the cassette tapes of Festivus past:

> **Frank**: *Alright, George. It's time for the feats of strength*
> **George**: *No! No! Turn it off! No feats of strength!*

The head of the family makes a choice as to who will participate in the Feats of Strength. However, a person may be allowed to decline the offer if they have something better to do instead:

> **Frank**: *This year, the honor goes to Mr. Kramer.*
> **Kramer**: *Uh-oh. Oh, gee, Frank, I'm sorry. I gotta go. I have to work a double shift at H&H.*

If the appointed person cannot participate, it is appropriate that

Andrew begins the feats of strength. Who won? Clearly, the spectators are enjoying the feat... they might be the real winners here.

another guest may nominate who should participate in the Feats of Strength:

> **George**: *Kramer! You can't go! Who's gonna do the feats of strength?*
> **Kruger**: *(Sipping liquor from a flask) How about George?*

Once the participants are identified, the "Feats of Strength" should begin with the head of household removing any bulky clothing and shouting the phrase "Let's Rumble", a la Frank Costanza:

> **Frank**: *(Removing his cardigan) Let's rumble!*

Classic Feats of Strength

Here we go... 1... 2... 3... wrestle! Traditionally, it is the head of the household that must be taken down and pinned. The victor will win bragging rights for the year to come, or at least until the party breaks up.

Depending on the size of the participants, you may need to move the furniture and depending on the ferocity of the participants, you may need medical personnel standing by. Always be prepared, and don't be afraid to consult a lawyer to prepare waivers if you feel that your guests may be of a litigious nature.

Some people may desire a Festivus celebration that does not require a post-party visit to the emergency room and/or long-term physiotherapy. In this case, you may want to avoid any particularly rigorous Feats of Strength.

There are plenty of excellent alternatives to a wrestling match... read on!

Arm Wrestling

Arm Wrestling is a great option. People likely won't sustain injuries other than a sore arm. An alternative idea is to have the

Arm Wrestling. A great alternative for your Festivus Feats of Strength.

participants use their non-dominant arm; i.e. right handed people use their left arm. You could organize a tournament, or simply nominate someone to take on the head of the household.

Thumb Wrestling

Some Festivus celebrations have adopted thumb wrestling as a suitable and safe feat of strength. Also referred to as a "thumb war", it is played by two competitors who use their thumbs to simulate fighting.

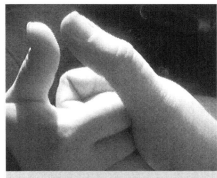

It can be a couple-friendly competition, as mild hand holding is involved. The players face each other and each holds out their right hand, or left hand, with their thumbs up. Then the participants link fingers in what is referred to as a "monkey grip".

1, 2, 3, 4... I declare a thumb war!

The game is typically initiated with both players repeating the rhyme "One, two, three, four, I declare a thumb war," and passing their thumb over their opponent's thumb in time with the rhyme. Immediately, on completion of the rhyme, the wrestling match begins. The winner is the player who can pin or hold the opponent's thumb down for a count of three.

Incidentally, some folks take thumb wrestling very seriously. There are competitive thumb wrestling leagues. In fact in an article, the *San Francisco Chronicle* referred to professional thumb wrestling as "the miniature golf of martial sports."[34]

You might also wish to add a tiny wrestling mask to your thumb to make it even zanier. You can purchase these masks online, or make your own. If you search the internet, you will find online videos that show you how to create a mask for your thumb. (Also useful for anonymous hitchhiking.)

Leg Wrestling

The opponents start by lying down on their backs, next to each other, but in opposite directions. They should be positioned so that their hips are next to each other. On the count of "one", each opponent raises their inside leg to a vertical position, then they drop their leg back down to the floor. On the count of "two", they repeat, raising their leg a second time, and then dropping it again. On "three", the opponents raise their legs, but this time they cross each other's leg and begin to wrestle. The goal is to apply the proper force on your opponent's leg in an attempt to flip them over backwards.

This is usually a less stressful physical activity than actual wrestling. A typical match ends quickly; it is more about tactics and gaining leverage than just brute strength. Make sure you have a large enough space available!

Other Low Impact Alternatives

Competition in the virtual world of a video game is a popular alternative. There are a variety you can choose from on all video

Blowing bubbles to mark Feats of Strength. Is this low impact enough for you?

game platforms. *Wii Bowling*, or *Wii Sports* is fun. You could even simulate actual wrestling through games available on both *Xbox* and *PlayStation*. *Rock Band* is very popular, however, at the moment an even more popular party video game is *Just Dance* (or its alternatives), which can be played by the entire family for hours on end. Now, the Feats of Strength will become the "Feats of Stamina"!

For a more relaxed time, try a party game. *Pictionary* or *Trivial Pursuit* can be a hoot. *Twister* can be fun for children or couples.

Board Games are fun for some. There is even a selection of *Seinfeld* themed board games such as *Seinfeld Clue* and *Seinfeld Monopoly* perfect for Festivus fun.

Poker could be just the thing, or a bar game such as darts may be popular. However, if it's drinking games you like I have two words for you... beer pong!

An outdoor Festivus could feature a horseshoe tournament, a tug-o-war or another picnic-style event such as a sack race, egg and spoon race or a three-legged race.

A tickle fight is a good alternative to real wrestling especially if there are small children at the gathering. Just send them to tickle the "head of the household" until he/she submits, then give the kids a treat for their efforts.

No idea what to do? Try seeing who can hold their breath the longest, or have a staring contest. Both less than exciting alternatives, but there is less stress and no contact involved.

Not Recommended!

- Anything to do with fire, including the lighting of farts.
- Anything that involves the rolling or riding of shopping carts down hills.
- Anything that involves the baiting or wrestling of wild animals.
- Anything that requires people to climb up on the roof.

Bear wrestling is not recommended! Just who do you think you are, Grizzly Adams?

- Anything that involves ingesting anything. Nickels can be poisonous if consumed in quantity.

The important thing is to have fun, not to figure out who is the biggest, strongest galoot of the bunch!

How do Other People Perform Feats of Strength?

In 2014, FestivusWeb.com asked its visitors to complete a survey and tell what they perform as Feats of Strength at their Festivus gathering. First, we discovered that only 62% of respondents said that they actually have Feats of Strength at Festivus-time, the remainder opting out of any sort of strenuous competition. Of those participating in Feats of Strength, a further 67% said there was "an attempt to pin the Head of the Household". It seems that a large portion of Festivus celebrants are honoring the tradition.

We also asked people to tell us about their specific Feats of Strength traditions. Some of the feedback we received is remarkable:

- Unwrapping of a package secured with duct tape. No knives allowed.
- Leg wrestling.
- We would see who could carry the largest person in attendance around the room.

- We have had arm, leg, or thumb wrestling. Mental games are also popular.

- We recognized opportunities as they arose such as opening jars, lifting the dog and or cat, moving the dining room table, etc.

Doesn't anyone try to overpower a team of horses anymore? Why not?

- We see who is able to cram the most marshmallow Christmas Peeps in his or her mouth.

- Limbo contest.

- Staring contest.

- We actually just sit around and watch WWE wrestling matches on the WWE network.

- A yoga plank off.

- We run an obstacle course in the backyard and attempt to lift each other up.

- People wrestle the dog.

- *Wii* Bowling.

- The "Opening of the Sauce Jar".

- Shredding of the Newspapers (for the fireplace).

- Beefarino eating contest.

- The head of the household wrestles the kids until they pin him or someone cries.

- Spitting contests.

- Beer can forehead-crushing contests.

- Just play wrestling with my daughters.

- Leg wrestling, but that lead to a full out wrestling match.

- Ripping of phone books.

- Arm wrestling with your weaker arm.

- Furniture moving competition, complete with the exclamation, "It's go time!"

The most popular Feats of Strength ideas turn out to be arm wrestling, thumb wrestling and just plain old wrestling; though many people did clarify that it was "play wrestling".

One of the most useful tips given was to ensure that the head of the household is sufficiently filled with meatloaf and other Festivus goodies, making him or her easier to pin. Historically, this is similar to the Roman Senators feeding Caesar a large plate of meatballs just prior to stabbing him to death.

Chapter 9 : Festivus Miracles

Although it is not an official element of the holiday or its celebration, the phenomenon of the Festivus Miracle was mentioned twice in the original episode, "The Strike".

As a result, the term "Festivus Miracle" has become widely accepted in popular culture.

Kramer's Two Miracles

In *Seinfeld*, it is Kramer who actually causes the occurrence of two "miracles".

Firstly, by inviting two off-track betting bookies to Festivus dinner (men whom Elaine wished to avoid):

> **Bookie**: *Hello again, Miss Benes.*
> **Elaine**: *What are you doing here?*
> **Bookie**: *Damnedest thing... me and Charlie were calling to ask you out, and, uh, we got this bagel place...*
> **Kramer**: *(Finishing the story) ...I told them I was just about to see you... It's a Festivus Miracle!*

Secondly, Kramer led Jerry's girlfriend Gwen to believe that Jerry was cheating on her, and then told Gwen where Jerry would be that evening:

> **Jerry**: *Gwen! How'd you know I was here?*
> **Gwen**: *Kramer told me.*
> **Kramer**: *Another Festivus Miracle!*

On these two occasions, Kramer enthusiastically declared it was a "Festivus Miracle", in an obvious parody of the popular holiday phrase "Christmas Miracle".

When asked about the origin of the term Festivus Miracle, Dan O'Keefe explained, "Festivus Miracle was something my dad used to say, but then I totally forgot about. Then, separately and independently, writer Dave Mandel pitched it for the episode."

Clearly another Festivus Miracle!

Festivus Miracles are All Around Us!

How popular is the term "Festivus Miracle" in today's society? If you search for the exact phrase "Festivus Miracle" in Google, you will receive about 54,000 results. You will also discover that many contemporary references to this phrase are found within the realms of sports, entertainment and politics.

Overall, the usage is quite broad. Any surprising occurrence, especially during the months of November and December, stands a good chance at being labeled a "Festivus Miracle".

Be alert for Festivus Miracles! They continue to appear in people's lives every year in and around the holiday season. Usually the appearances are just as lame and as forced as Kramer's miracles. However, when people use the phrase, "It's a Festivus Miracle", just about anything may seem special...

> **Oliver**: *Gas went down 12 cents...*
> **Stan**: *It's a Festivus Miracle!*
>
> **Lucy**: *I found the TV remote...*
> **Ricky**: *It's a Festivus Miracle!*
>
> **Martin**: *I hit every green light on the way to work...*
> **Lewis**: *It's a Festivus Miracle!*

Don't be afraid to use it liberally! You won't regret it.

Chapter 10 : The Human Fund

What's the deal with "The Human Fund"? Have you heard of this thing?

Seriously, the Human Fund is the name of a fake charity that was used by George Costanza on donation cards he gave to his co-workers at Kruger Industrial Smoothing.

He devised the idea after getting a similar gift from his friend Tim Whatley, who gave out cards that stated, "This holiday season a donation has been made in your name to the Children's Alliance." George's response was, "I got him Yankee's tickets! He got me a piece of paper saying 'I've given your gift to someone else!'"

While George was perturbed by Whatley's gift, it gave him the idea to do the same. The only difference is that George's charity, The Human Fund, was invented. He even conceived a fake slogan for the charity, "Money For People".

 To celebrate the holiday season a donation has been made in your name to:

The Human Fund
"Money for People"

Happy Festivus!

It was such a good scam it completely fooled everyone at his workplace, including George's boss, Mr. Kruger, who gave George a company check for $20,000 to be donated to "The Human Fund". Later, after the accounting department figured out the ruse, Kruger challenged George into admitting the charity didn't exist. This caused a chain of events that saw George having to invite Kruger to his family's Festivus celebration.

How did the Idea Arise?

Seinfeld writer Jeff Schafer has said that the invention of the Human Fund was based on real life events. "Every year we would get a Christmas card from *Castle Rock*," Schafer reported.[35] Apparently, *Castle Rock*'s card also had the phrase, "A donation was made in your name..." Schafer actually used this phrase as the stimulus to write the Human Fund gag into "The Strike".

How Popular is this Meme?

To this day, you will find plenty of references to the Human Fund in our society. A Google search for the phrase "Human Fund" brings up approximately 43,000 results. Users will find dozens of references to *Seinfeld* as well as images of Human Fund cards people have created and used as a gag with their friends and coworkers.

There is a legitimate organization named "The Human Fund" based in Cleveland, Ohio, that drew its name from the *Seinfeld* episode. The charity supports arts education programs for the under-served youth of the city of Cleveland.

Finally, in the *Lost* television show episode "Everybody Loves Hugo" the character Hugo Reyes (Hurley), after being presented with an prestigious award, sends-up *Seinfeld* when he tells his mother that they have an upcoming event with the "Human Fund".

Chapter 11 : Festivus Party Ideas

Keep in mind, as with the O'Keefes and the Costanzas, Festivus is something that should occur naturally, based on the whim of the host and the cooperation of the guests. This should always be considered when you adopt this holiday. Do it the way you want; don't worry about how others do it. If you see something fun that others are doing, then adopt it and make it your own... and have fun! Or don't... it's up to you because it's a holiday for the rest of us. That means you! It's your day!

The traditional date of Festivus is December 23. However, many people do not worry about having their celebration on the "official" date. If you are planning to host a Festivus Party, don't be worried about choosing a different date in December, or any other day of the year for that matter.

Fun Festivus Party Ideas

We have a few proven ideas for you to incorporate extra fun into your Festivus...

Seinfeld Potluck

Ask your guests to bring food items of their choice, but for additional fun the food should have some connection to the *Seinfeld* series. There can be a lot of creativity and fun had by trying to figure out a good dish made with "Hampton Tomatoes", or you could bring a big bowl of "Lobster Bisque" or a paper sack filled with "Calzone". We have a long list of suggestions in Appendix A.

In the author's family, this disturbing poodle statuette is regifted every year, turning the excitement of opening a gift into a terrifying surprise for whichever victim receives the package.

Regift Exchange

Instead of going out and buying gifts to exchange, tell everyone to bring an item to regift, which is taking a gift that has been received in the past, rewrapping it and bringing it to the party. Of course, the idea of regifting is another Seinfeldism taken from the episode "The Label Maker" *(S06E12)*. The worse the gift, the more the fun. The exchange could be done using our fun Regift Exchange Script which is included in Appendix B. It can make the gift exchange more fun and interactive.

Seinfeld Costume Party

Ask your guests to dress up as a character from *Seinfeld*. This is a lot more work for the guests but it will pay off in hilarity. Make sure you offer prizes for the best costumes.

Party Favors

You can give out party favors to spark everyone's mood. Some good ideas we've seen are Pez dispensers, individually wrapped black and white cookies, "Human Fund" cards, individual serving size boxes of cereal or goldfish crackers in a baggie.

Assign Someone to Bring the Pole

When you are inviting a similar group of guests to an annual Festivus party, you might assign a different person to provide the Festivus pole each year. The notion is that each annual assignee will be challenged to bring something even more unique and/or hilarious than what was brought the previous year.

A Grieving Pole

For the Airing of Grievances, you could pass around a small replica of a Festivus pole as a "grieving pole". Decree that whoever holds the pole gets to air their grievances. A short metal rod will suffice.

Ugly Sweater Party

Yes, it's a crossover from a popular Christmas party tradition but there is nothing more hilarious than a pack of people all wearing ugly sweaters. So why not?

Elaine-style Dance Off

A fun party event might be an Elaine-style dance off, especially if you enjoy watching people who appear to be having a full body dry heave set to music. You might want to play "Shining Star" by Earth, Wind & Fire to make it even more authentic. Again, you should offer prizes. May we suggest a selection of delicious Jujyfruits or a case of Today sponges?

Kramer Entrance Contest

Get the contestants to enter the room through a nearby door. Judges could score based on body movement, footwork and facial expression. We leave the idea of the prize up to you. It could be anything, as Kramer loves everything.

Puffy Shirt Party

Get everyone to wear a puffy shirt. Make sure you have some fancy frills and safety pins on hand to decorate the shirts of any party-poopers who show up in landlubber clothing. Don't

Who has the thickest wallet? Give them a murse.

pay attention to them if they say, "I don't want to be a pirate!" Just reply, "Avast ye matey", and then force them to conform.

Thickest Wallet Contest

You know how men like to measure things and brag about size? This could easily be a hit at your next Festivus party! Just break out a ruler and see who has the thickest wallet. The prize could be a "European Carry-All", or as some refer to it, a "murse".

Seinfeld Trivia

A popular choice! Everybody loves a little trivia competition. You could have a formal British pub-style trivia night, with a quizmaster and teams, or you could host something more informal. You could also look into getting your hands on a *Seinfeld* trivia game such as *Scene-it Seinfeld Edition* or the *Seinfeld Trivia* board game, as it saves you from the task of inventing the questions. However, one warning! You might have *Seinfeld* experts mixed in with *Seinfeld* newcomers. You should consider having advanced questions for the experts in the group.

Seinfeldisms

Any good Festivus party must be rife with Seinfeldisms. Making a few *Seinfeld* references is a great way to get everyone in the mood for fun. How important are Seinfeldisms? Important! We've got an entire chapter about it later on in this book (if you could possibly keep reading beyond this point...).

Consider a small gesture, such as referring to guests as "Shmoopie" when they arrive for your party. How about putting a sign on the pretzel bowl that says, "These pretzels are making me thirsty!"

If even that's too much, consider creating "New York City" nametags for guests. You don't think it's a good idea? We don't think it's so bad. People should wear nametags; everyone would be a lot friendlier. "Hello, Sam! How are you doing, Joe?" See how friendly it is!

As a potential Festivus party host, please consider these exchanges as examples of the type of behavior we are

A simple notecard placed in front of a pretzel bowl will both serve as a warning to your dry-mouthed guests, and titillate any *Seinfeld* fans in attendance.

referring to:

> **Guest**: *They opened a new Chinese Restaurant in my neighborhood.*
> **Host**: *Do they make you wait forever, then call out Cartwright when they need you?*
> **Guest**: *(Strange look)*
>
> **Guest**: *I brought my car into the shop.*
> **Host**: *Did the mechanic kidnap it and drive it to Michigan?*
> **Guest**: *(Strange look)*
>
> **Guest**: *I have a new mailman.*
> **Host**: *Is he addicted to Chunky bars and Kenny Rogers chicken?*
> **Guest**: *(Strange look)*

If your guests weren't *Seinfeld* fans before the party, they will be by the time it's over. On the other hand, they just may leave confused, hating you and *Seinfeld* forever.

Chapter 12 : The Songs of Festivus

The traditional *Seinfeld* Festivus, as depicted in "The Strike", did not include any music or songs. It would have been nice to see Frank and Estelle Costanza lead the gathering in a heartfelt rendition of "O Festivus", but it just never happened. (Take it up with the *Seinfeld* writers!)

While the *Seinfeld* version of the holiday is barren of tunes, there are plenty of references to music in the original version of the holiday. The O'Keefe family had a selection of songs the family performed at their annual Festivus celebration. In his book, *The Real Festivus*, a humorous Dan O'Keefe describes it as "Irish Death Music".

Since Festivus has become more popular, there have been a few Festivus songs written and performed. Many of these are to the tune of well-known Christmas carols and other Christmas-related songs.

Meet Joel Kopischke

If you have grown weary of the old holiday songs, then check out Joel Kopischke, a Milwaukee native who has a whole repertoire of humorous holiday music, including a pair of songs about our favorite holiday. Joel's humorous holiday release *I Got Yule Babe* (http://igotyulebabe.com) has been heard on *XM Radio*, *DIRECTV* and *The Dr. Demento Show*, and includes the track "'O Festivus", his first Festivus related recording.

When Canadians first hear "O Festivus" it might move them. In fact, it may make them remove their hats and stand at attention. When people sing this song, they should just

O Festivus!

(Sung to the tune of "O Canada")

O Festivus!
Your praises now we sing,
For the rest of us,
there will be no re-gifting

Thy shining pole of aluminum
Completely tinsel-free

We air grievances,
Oh Festivus,
can you spare a square for me?

Thy feats of strength,
are must see TV
Frank Costanza,
we'll pin you first, you'll see

Oh Festivus,
you are sponge worthy

(Parody lyrics by Joel Kopischke)

imagine they are at a hockey game and it's Festivus day.

Another of Kopischke's songs, "The Festivus Bunch", from his album *Ground Control to Santa Claus* (http://groundcontroltosantaclaus.com) is a send-up to *The Brady Bunch* theme song... "Then this one day when the show was on the TV... and they saw it caused so much of a fuss...". Would you like to keep singing along? Full lyrics are included on Page 41.

Joel is a Wisconsinite. Strangely enough, throughout our search for the meaning of Festivus, we seem to stumble across Wisconsin references again and again. When we asked Joel about the connection between Wisconsin and Festivus, he responded "Wisconsinites have a great sense of humor, first of all. And the idea of Festivus is pretty dang funny."

Further to this, Joel seems to have a perfect understanding of our favorite holiday:

"Holidays have ritualized traditions that almost no one knows or understands the meaning or the history of, so any holiday tradition, when taken out of context can seem totally random and odd. Festivus shines a light on that. Why is an unadorned aluminum pole any more ridiculous than a conifer bedecked with lights and ornaments and popcorn and tinsel? It's not, except that our cultural traditions say one is normal and one is crazy. Additionally in all great humor there is an element of truth, and what holidays usually mean is getting together with family, for good or bad. Festivus takes the metaphorical struggles we have with our relatives and heightens them to a real physical wrestling match, and takes the things we mutter under our breath, turns up the volume and airs those grievances!"

When asked if he was planning any more Festivus song parodies, Joel immediately responded with a brand new song, just for this book! It's sung to the tune of "O Hanukkah O Hanukkah", and may well be included on one of Joel's future releases:

O Festivus, O Festivus!

O Festivus, O Festivus
We can't overrate ya
When even Jewish
Folks celebrate ya

It came to us from Seinfeld
Still seen on cable
The episode "The Strike"
With Kramer and the bagels

No tree nor
Menorah
It's just an aluminum pole
No tinsel in fact
That would only distract
It's got a high strength-to-weight ratio

O Festivus for the rest of us
We all celebrate ya
With airing of the grievances
Your relatives berate ya

And with the feats of strength
The holiday won't end
Until the head of household
We manage to pin

Festivus
Festivus
If you're sincere or satirical
Forget all the rest
It's the holiday that's best
And that's the Festivus miracle!

Sung to the tune of "O Hanukkah, O Hanukkah!"
Parody lyrics by Joel Kopischke

FestivusWeb.com Songbook

Most Festivus songs stay true to the humor of the holiday. Beginning in 2010, FestivusWeb.com has been posting Festivus-based lyrics to a few holiday favorites. Families around the world can now croon about Festivus around the aluminum pole, or at the dinner table. They can even serenade the Feats of Strength loser while they are at the hospital emergency room. If you are a true Festivus fan you should be singing these songs loudly and proudly, at least until your family complains thrice.

It's Festivus all Across the Land

(Sung to the tune of "Winter Wonderland")

Grievances aired, are you listening,
At the dinner, meatloaf is glistening.
A beautiful sight, we're happy tonight.
It's Festivus all across the land.

Standing there, is an old pole,
Unadorned, it's a strong pole.
It stands straight and tall,
As we go along,
It's Festivus all across the land.

In the living room we can wrestle,
And try to pin the head of the house.
He'll say: Are you ready?
We'll say: No, man.
But we will do our best
To pin him down.

Later on, we'll conspire,
As we air grievances by the fire.
To face unafraid,
The gripes we have made,
It's Festivus all across the land.

It's a Pole

(Sung to the tune of 'Let it Snow')

Oh the Festivus party is starting,
And the guests are just arriving.
What's that thing over there?
It's a pole! It's a pole! It's a pole!

It doesn't require decorating,
Because tinsel is way too distracting.
It's unadorned and made of aluminum,
It's a pole! It's a pole! It's a pole!

Finally we air our grievances,
There are problems with all you people.
But if you really do it right,
Somebody will be sobbing tonight.

There's still more fun to unfold,
Cause it's time to pin the head of the household.
The feats of strength will happen now!
Move the pole! Move the pole! Move the pole!

The Festivus Song

(Grievances Aired at a Festivus Party)

(Sung to the tune of "The Christmas Song")
(ie. Chestnuts Roasting on an Open Fire)

Grievances aired at a Festivus Party,
Feats of strength, and a bloody nose.
Random miracles make Kramer's day,
As Festivus newcomers come and go.

Everybody knows of the pole without tinsel,
It's less distracting that way.
Let's play the tapes from Festivus past,
And embarrass George til he runs away.

We all know that Frank Costanza loves this day,
No more fighting over dolls in any way.

It's every crazy fathers true delight,
To challenge his son in a weird Festivus fight!

And so we are offering you this simple day,
To people who love crazy things.
It should only be said, in one simple way,
Happy Festivus, to you!

Dreaming of a Happy Festivus

(Sung to the tune of White Christmas)

I'm dreaming of a Happy Festivus
Just like the ones we used to know.
Where the pole has no tinsel,
And the guests will all listen,
To hear grievances aired to one and all.

I'm dreaming of a Happy Festivus,
With every Festivus grievance that I write.
May your aluminum pole stand upright,
And may Festivus fun last all night.
May your aluminum pole stand upright,
And may Festivus fun last all night.

O Festivus

(Sung to the tune of 'O Christmas Tree')

O Festivus, O Festivus,
Costanza's day, for the rest of us.
An aluminum pole, it's tinsel free,
And feats of strength, who can pin me?

O Festivus, O Festivus,
Costanza's day, for the rest of us.
No raining blows, for sake of a doll,
Just grievances, aired to one and all.

O Festivus, O Festivus,
Costanza's day, for the rest of us!

The Twelve Days of Festivus

On the first day of Festivus, my Seinfeld gave to me...
A pole that's tinsel free.

On the second day of Festivus, my Seinfeld gave to me...
2 Festivus miracles
And a pole that's tinsel free.

On the third day of Festivus, my Seinfeld gave to me...
3 Fake phone numbers
2 Festivus miracles
And a pole that's tinsel free.

On the fourth day of Festivus, my Seinfeld gave to me...
4 Unexpected newcomers
3 Fake phone numbers
2 Festivus miracles
And a pole that's tinsel free.

On the fifth day of Festivus, my Seinfeld gave to me...
5 Grievances Aired
4 Unexpected newcomers
3 Fake phone numbers
2 Festivus miracles
And a pole that's tinsel free.

(and the rest...)

Sixth Day.:   6 Shvitz hours

Seventh Day: 7 Face changes

Eigth Day: 8 Blows rained

Ninth Day: 9 Day-old bagels

Tenth Day: 10 Bucks on Captain Nemo

Eleventh Day: 11 Human Fund Donations

Twelfth Day: 12 Years on Strike

Silver Poles

(Sung to the tune of 'Silver Bells')

Silver poles, silver poles
It's Festivus at the Costanza's
see them shine, yours and mine
soon it will be Festivus night

Chops of mutton, be a glutton
Have a slice of meatloaf
And save room for some
Marble rye bread

This is Festivus
For the rest of us
It's Costanza's big scene
And without all the tinsel
You'll see

Silver poles, silver poles
It's Festivus at the Costanza's
see them shine, yours and mine
soon it will be Festivus night

Lots of problems, feats of strength
Pinning heads of households
In the air
There's a feeling
of Festivus

Children crying
People fighting
Drinking booze from a flask
And in the living room you'll see

Silver poles, silver poles
It's Festivus in the city
see them shine, yours and mine
soon it will be Festivus night

(Parody lyrics by Lynn Gibson)

Chapter 13 : Festivus Tips

By now, you probably understand that most people view Festivus as a fun, zany time. In this chapter, we present some important tips to make your Festivus even more hilarious. Enjoy!

Tip #1: Don't perform the Feats of Strength with Grandpa. His place smells like potatoes and so does he.

That's a lot of potatoes!

Tip #2: Always dress appropriately for Festivus. A denim vest with snaps can be considered too casual. A nice puffy shirt is more formal but you can be sure that people will heckle you with "Avast ye matey"! - there's no comeback for that! Maybe a Technicolor Dreamcoat and a furry pimp hat would be the best way to go!

Tip #3: It's okay to cry before, during and after the Feats of Strength. Don't feel bad! A lot of people tend to cry when they see two out of shape grown-ups smash their bodies together.

Tip #4: When preparing a well-balanced Festivus feast, keep in mind that Jujyfruits is not really fruit and marble rye should not actually be served on a fishing pole.

Tip #5: When Festivus is near, always be on the lookout for Festivus miracles. Did a parking spot open up right in front of you? Did the candy machine drop two Twix bars when you only paid for one? Did your fear of clowns give you an excuse for skipping a trip to the circus with the kids? These all count.

Tip #6: Airing your Grievances can be cleansing for your soul, but think about holding back on certain complaints, such as Grandma's clicking dentures that sound like "La Cucaracha", Uncle Jim's National Guard war stories or Cousin Tim's amazing unibrow.

Tip #7: If you are serving paella at your Festivus gathering, make sure you don't make too much. You don't want too much! Then you'll be wondering, "What am I supposed to do with all this paella?" Also, make sure you serve some cake after the meal. Who doesn't serve cake after a meal? What kind of people? Would  it kill people to put out a pound cake? Something! You don't want to have people sitting there like idiots drinking coffee without a piece of cake!

Tip #8: If you are shy, anonymously write your grievances on a sticky note and post the note on the Festivus pole. You don't have to sign your name but you can always put the phone number of the off-track betting place or the local bagel shop just to throw people off.

Tip #9: When looking for old crap to regift at Festivus, don't overlook the obvious: The Waterpik you won in a computer sales contest, all that extra Chinese gum you accidentally bought, or a "Cigar Store Indian" you once thought was "kitschy". What about that Label Baby Jr.? Stick a "Happy Festivus" label on it and throw it on the pile!

Tip #10: Small talk is important at any gathering. Try not to insult anyone who may or may not have had a pony growing up. Also, if anyone asks about the hen, the chicken, and the rooster... they're all the same animal and they're all having sex with each other. You might think it's perverse, but that's just the way it is.

Tip #11: When the Airing of Grievances occurs, someone may throw a real doozy at you. Whatever it is, you may wish to avoid the subject altogether. Try to throw them off by telling them that you have a gum guy. Tell them that you have a friend in the gum business and if you make one phone call, boxes of gum will be delivered right to

their door. If that doesn't work, try doing some Jose Jimenez impressions... or promise to get them an autograph of Keith Hernandez.

Tip #12: Festivus is not over until the head of the household is pinned. In wrestling, they have a referee, so it might be a good idea to appoint someone as a referee at your Festivus gathering. But don't use Granny, she really enjoys it when there is a good tussle. She'll probably never declare the match over.

Tip #13: When preparing to air your grievances, you might be wise to make notecards. What's more embarrassing: losing your train of thought or standing in front of everybody reading from notecards?

Tip #14: It is customary for some people to record the Festivus proceedings on tape. However, many people will not talk if they know a tape recorder is running. So, secretly place the tape recorder in a locked briefcase. Keep in mind you can also store soda crackers in the briefcase in case you need a quick snack.

Tip #15: Try to avoid disappointment by checking your wagers before you attend the Festivus gathering. Your horse may have won, or he/she may have done so poorly that they had to be shot. Mourning a dead racehorse will surely put a damper on the festivities.

Be warned... any sort of pole-like object can attract pole dancers.

Tip #16: December 23rd may be the official day for celebrating Festivus but you can celebrate Festivus any time you like. After all, Festivus is all about convenience. For example, if the kids are begging to go to the water park, or if your in-laws want you to come over for a visit, tell them they can't... because it's Festivus. Similarly, if your significant other tells you that they're not in the mood, tell them that it's a special occasion... Festivus!

Tip #17: Make sure your Festivus pole is plain and unadorned. If it is too glitzy it may attract adult entertainers!

Tip #18: Prior to performing the Feats of Strength be sure to sufficiently warm up and stretch your muscles. This is an important step. You don't want to pull anything! Of course, the warm up period could last all night, or at least until your opponent loses interest.

Save the whale George. Save it for me...

Tip #19: If someone invites you to a Festivus party at the beach... never, ever, ever tell anyone that you're a marine biologist.

Tip #20: If you are challenged to feats of strength, you could say, "I choose not to wrestle!" However, if the person finally goads you into it, you could try to begin wrestling a few seconds before the referee says "go". This will likely give you the edge you need to win the bout.

Chapter 14 : The Manifestations of Festivus

Since December 1997, Festivus has appeared in many facets of mainstream society. On some occasions the entire concept of Festivus is used as a theme. On other times the Festivus name is only borrowed to endorse products and services.

Festivus and its motif has appeared in colleges, on media such as television and the internet, retold in books, displayed in public squares, regurgitated in politics and featured as the name of dozens of events ranging from film festivals to sled races. Let's take a look!

Colleges and Universities

Festivus has been an entity at college dorms and fraternities for over a decade now. Even today, with the new generation of students not having as intimate a knowledge of *Seinfeld* as previous ones, they still seem to understand the nature of Festivus.

Students at the University of Wisconsin-Madison first held a Festivus celebration in 2003. It continued to be held in subsequent years, growing to about 300 participants in 2004 and 500 in 2005.

In 2004, the University of Richmond renamed their annual pig roast event "Festivus" as part of a concerted effort to change the event's tarnished image.

In 2005, Drew University in Madison, New Jersey, held a midnight breakfast during exam week in celebration of Festivus. It included all the main elements of Festivus; an aluminum pole, feats of strength, and airing of grievances.

In 2006, Columbia University's Living-Learning Center held a Festivus celebration during first semester finals.

At Elon University, a private liberal arts university in Elon, North Carolina, students have been celebrating Festivus since 2005. The Elon University Festivus party does not normally feature airing of grievances or a Festivus pole. Its main connection to Festivus is the notion of a "Festivus for the Rest of Us". While college students normally socialize in cliques segregated by dorms and fraternities, Festivus is college-wide and open to everyone! This makes it one of the most popular and well-attended parties on campus. The party is notorious as an orgy of excess. Held outdoors in April just prior to final exams, it features dozens of beer kegs, roast pigs and a giant pool of mud meant for wrestling. The result is filthy mayhem.

At Connecticut College in New London, Connecticut, the annual Festivus celebration has become a college mainstay. The campus-wide party, usually held in December about two weeks before exams, provides a chance for students to let their hair down before the crush of final exams. The one important element that is borrowed from *Seinfeld* is that the party is a non-denominational celebration. This is important as it allows everyone to celebrate together. As well as a huge campus-wide dance, each residence hall hosts its own Festivus party, usually featuring traditional elements of Festivus such as aluminum poles, airing of grievances and feats of strength. Traditions are always changing, but Festivus at Connecticut College is one that has been a constant over the years.

Students at Briar Cliff University, a small Liberal Arts college in Sioux City, Iowa, celebrate Festivus as a large year-ending party. Usually held in April, it involves a large portion of the student population who camp out and celebrate three straight days.

In November 2010, and again in 2011, "Festivus, A Latin Celebration!" was held at Rhodes College in Memphis, Tennessee. Designed for high school students, participants enjoy contests, games, feats of strength, and lectures from Rhodes faculty and admissions counselors.

Public Institutions

In 2005, the Baltimore, Maryland Department of Public Works release their 2006 calendar, which included a "Festivus Appreciation Day" on December 23rd. To the surprise of Baltimoreans, the calendar also included a picture of a Festivus pole.

In 2007, Green Bay, Wisconsin resident Sean Ryan requested that a Festivus pole be erected at Green Bay's City Hall. His tongue-in-cheek request was made just after the go ahead was given to place a nativity scene at the same location.

In 2008-2010, the Adams Morgan Business Improvement District in Washington, D.C. held an "airing of grievances" on bulletin boards that were located in a special kiosk. The grievances were later "aired" by a town crier in a jester hat

Many grievances were aired at the Festivus kiosk in the Adams Morgan District, Washington, DC.

the following weekend. The tradition lasted three years before it was discontinued, as the organizers felt it had run its course.

In 2010, Malcolm King, an inmate at the Theo Lacy Jail in Santa Ana, California, requested special meals for his "Festivus" faith. He was given "kosher" non-salami meals for two months while the county worked through the legal system to get the decision thrown out, arguing that kosher meals and religious observances were not a part of Festivus. However, the entire issue dissolved in October 2010, when King was released from the jail.

Food, Wine and Beer

In 2000, only two years after the original episode aired, Ben and Jerry's introduced an ice cream variety named "Festivus (a holiday for the rest of us)". Available in a limited batch, it consisted of brown sugar-cinnamon ice cream mixed with gingerbread cookie chunks and a ginger caramel swirl. *Seinfeld* writer Dan O'Keefe later remarked, "It seems odd that a family holiday became an ice cream."[36] As much as its existence was truly a Festivus miracle, the flavor was discontinued after only one year. Requests for its resurgence continue to this day.

You probably thought that "PBR" was the beer of Festivus... think again. There are many more choices out there, especially in the worlds of craft beer and microbreweries. For example, if you are in Philadelphia, PA you might imbibe in "Manayunk Festivus Ale" available from the Manayunk Brewing Company. Brewed with cardamom and brown sugar, it has a spicy, raisin flavor. It is sold in cans, and at 7% alcohol by volume, it's a much stronger brew than your average can of PBR. Be careful... this is how uncles become drunk uncles.

Some other Festivus beer offerings you might try are "Festivus Ale" by Hamilton Creek Brewery in Nashville Tennessee, "Festivus" winter warmer from the Full Pint Brewing Company in North Versailles, Pennsylvania or a pint of "Festivus" at the Minneapolis Town Hall Brewery in Minneapolis, Minnesota.

If you find yourself in Colorado, you might attend a popular

Festivus-themed craft beer festival featuring over forty breweries. The "Denver Beer Festivus" has been in existence since 2011, and has become an annual December tradition.

If beer is not your favorite, there have also been several offerings of Festivus-themed wines. In 2004, Grape Ranch Vineyards in Okemah, Oklahoma began to produce "Festivus Red", a holiday wine. In 2006, Pedroncelli Winery, in Geyserville, California, produced a Festivus wine. The 2003 Cabernet Sauvignon was billed as "a wine to toast grievances by to embolden your most bodacious feats of strength."

Online

It was back on 23 August, 2003, when a page titled "Festivus" was first added to *Wikipedia* by user "Ark30inf". The text of the inaugural page, which summarized the *Seinfeld* version of Festivus, was only 175 words.

Since then there has been a continuous surge of Festivus activity online. Every year brings more people to Festivus and generates additional online traffic. On *Twitter*, Festivus is a trending topic that usually peaks on the 23rd of December. Hash tags such as #AiringofGrievances and #FestivusMiracle trend on the days in and around December 23rd. Several *Facebook* fan pages, such as "facebook.com/ICelebrateFestivus" and "facebook.com/Festivuspoles" light up with traffic during the run-up to Festivus. *Tumblr* and *Instagram* are also used to share Festivus related photos and to build excitement leading up to December 23rd.

In a December 2010 article, the *Christian Science Monitor* reported that Festivus had become a top trend on Twitter.[37] It may be true, as *Seinfeld* writer Dan O'Keefe had predicted, "half of what's clogging up the Internet is porn and the other half is references to Festivus."[38]

In 2012, *Google* began to feature an aluminum pole on the left side of their search results page for the search term "festivus". The exclamation "A festivus miracle!" is a prefix for the results count near the top of the page. *CNET* referred to the Easter egg as, "a pure, unadorned, no-pressure Festivus pole. It's handy if you don't happen to have one of your own."[39]

Books

There have been three books published about Festivus.

The Real Festivus, written by Dan O'Keefe, was released on 1 November 2005. It details the O'Keefe family Festivus, and dispels many notions about the origin of the holiday. It also featured an introduction by Jason Alexander.

Also released in 2005 was writer Allen Salkin's *Festivus. The Holiday for the Rest of Us*. Republished in 2008, this successful book served to further popularize the holiday. Dan O'Keefe however, lambasted the book, most significantly in a *Washington Post* online chat where he referred to the book's author very negatively.[40] In addition Larry O'Keefe, middle son of the O'Keefe family, said the book was "filled with misinformation and lies."[41] Certainly, some of the umbrage might have been caused by Salkin's angle that Festivus existed long before Daniel O'Keefe Sr. invented it, something that has been wholly refuted by members of the O'Keefe family. They are more than confident their father created Festivus all on his own. On the other hand, the negative reviews may have resulted from Salkin's insulting description of Dan O'Keefe's hair.

In 2015, this very book was released. *Festivus! The Book* is meant as a useful (if not humorous) reference that serves to summarize and recap the integration of Festivus into modern society. Hope you are enjoying it!

Politics

In 2005, Wisconsin Governor Jim Doyle displayed a Festivus pole in the family room of the Executive Residence in Madison, Wisconsin. Today, Governor Doyle's famous 2005 Festivus pole is now part of the collection of the Wisconsin Historical Museum.

In 2008, while he was attending Governor Rod Blagojevich's

impeachment hearings in the Illinois state Capitol, teenager Michael Tennenhouse stumbled upon a collection of holiday displays, including a nativity scene and a menorah. Being a *Seinfeld* fan, he applied for a permit and won the right to place a Festivus pole (actually a pool skimmer pole) on display in the Capitol Building. Tennenhouse's motive was stated as an "airing of grievances" on behalf of the people of Illinois with respect to Governor Rod Blagojevich. Afterward, the media began to refer to the special committee of Illinois House lawmakers deciding Blagojevich's fate as "airing grievances" against the embattled Illinois Governor.

On 23 December 2013, Greg Gordon organized a group that performed an airing of grievances at the Wisconsin Capitol. The complaints were mostly aimed at Governor Scott Walker and his policies, however other gripes were about a lack of eggnog, homelessness, the size of beer glasses, disappointment in not winning the lottery and media censorship.

In December of 2013 and 2014, Kentucky Senator Rand Paul celebrated Festivus with a series of Festivus-related tweets. In a series of politically motivated (140-character or less) rants he expressed his discontent with wasteful spending, poked fun at other Senators, blasted the media and teased the public by hinting at a 2016 Presidential run.

Sports and Fitness

In Baltimore, Festivus has been synonymous with the Baltimore Raven's playoff chances and/or winning the Super Bowl for the past fifteen years. Beginning in the fall of 2000 as the NFL season neared the end, Coach Brian Billick forbade anyone to speak the word "playoffs". Instead, Ravens players and fans began to use the term "Festivus". In addition, "Festivus Maximus" became the nickname for the Super Bowl. The Ravens actually went on to win the Super Bowl that year, which is why superstitious fans continue to embrace the tradition to this day.

In 2010, a minor league baseball team used Festivus as a game day promotion for their June 26th game. The West Michigan Whitecaps honored Festivus with a "Table of Grievances", Feats of Strength, a Festivus pole and on-field contests including trivia, a minute-to-win-it Festivus cake-eating contest and a Feats of Strength hula-hoop contest. Based on the success of that promotion, other minor league baseball teams have been following suit. On July 7th 2011, the Bowie Baysox of Bowie, Maryland held a Festivus Night in their Prince George's Stadium. Fans shared Festivus tidings around a traditional Festivus pole on the concourse level of the stadium. As well, they took part in *Seinfeld* trivia and a Kramer look-alike contest.

Founded in 2011, "Festivus Games" is a CrossFit style competition featuring athletic feats of strength and endurance for novice and intermediate athletes. It's billed as "The Games for the Rest of Us", meaning that it is a competition where budding and amateur athletes may be measured against their peers. Once a small competition of only 70 athletes, it is now a North American-wide competition involving over one hundred fitness clubs and nearly 5,000 athletes.

Have you heard of frisbee golf? It's called "frolf" and it's a perfect sport for something called the "Summer of George". At frolf courses in both Adair, Oregon and Virginia Beach, Virginia, local frolf tournaments have been named after Festivus.

Television

An episode of *Jeopardy!* from 2004 featured a *Seinfeld*-theme. The category named "Festivus" required contestants to answer questions about holidays. Incidentally, this was the final episode in the initial record setting run of long-time champion Ken Jennings.

During the 2013 and 2014 annual Christmas episodes of *The Simpsons*, the animators gave a nod to Festivus in the opening "Couch Gag". On both occasions, the character Comic Book Guy was shown standing with an aluminum pole and a multi-colored "Festivus" banner. When they did it in 2013, Festivus fans said, "Cowabunga!" When they did it again in 2014, they said, "Best repeat of a secular holiday reference ever!"

Music Industry

In 2005, the popular Glen Rock, New Jersey punk/indie rock band Titus Andronicus named their debut album *The Airing of Grievances*.

Wale, a popular Nigerian-American rapper from Washington, D.C. "dropped" a mixtape named *Festivus* on 23 December 2014. The promotional art featured an old style cassette recorder, similar to the one Frank Costanza played in the diner on the *Seinfeld* episode "The Strike". In addition, the tracks have profusely sampled audio from *Seinfeld*. The Festivus mixtape was done as a promotion for his upcoming album titled *The Album About Nothing*, clearly a send-up to *Seinfeld*. Are rap fans also *Seinfeld* fans? Maybe Wale is onto something.

Everywhere Else...

In 2007, members of the Saint Louis Adventure Group began to hold an annual Festivus party that continues to the present day. It has been referred to as one of the most successful public Festivus celebrations ever. Since 2011, it has been held at Kirkwood Station Brewing Company, in Kirkwood, Missouri.

Between 2008 and 2012, the "Festivus Film Festival" was held in Denver, Colorado. Nicknamed "the film fest for the rest of us", the annual January festival highlighted "truly independent" films and filmmakers.

At the Freret Market in New Orleans, an annual event named "Freretstivus" is held. A "Regifting Booth" is setup, where you bring something you hate and exchange it for something you like. Afterward, guests are invited to attach a grievance to the pole at the "Office of Homeland Serenity."

In Battle Creek, Michigan, the BCMAMS (Battle Creek

The Frank Costanza action figure by *Vinyl Sugar* released just in time for Festivus 2015!

Metropolitan Area Moustache Society) holds an annual Festivus sled race. The challenge to participants is to build their own sled using only cardboard, paint and adhesive. For non-sledders the event also includes a chili cook-off, an ugly sweater competition, geocaching and horse-drawn sleigh rides. The event was first held in 2009, and continues to this day.

In July 2015, *Vinyl Sugar* released a line of *Seinfeld* action figures featuring an 8-inch "Frank Costanza" figure depicted grasping his iconic aluminum pole. Another Festivus miracle!

Finally, a reason to head up to your moth-infested attic and rescue your long forgotten "cabana wear". In 2014, *Norwegian Cruise Lines* advertised "Festivus Cruises". Billed as a Festivus miracle, they did not actually promise a Festivus pole. However, they did offer gingerbread making contests and special menu items. We're sure they must have had meatloaf available at the midnight buffet.

Chapter 15 : It's Festivus Everywhere!

Have you ever wondered how others actually celebrate Festivus? We can usually learn from others' experiences, which is why we spent significant effort asking people to tell us all about their Festivus celebrations. Some folks ran away and hid! However, a few brave souls did agree to participate in our quest for knowledge. Thank you very much for sharing your stories.

Now, sit back, relax, and read about Festivus... everywhere.

Festivus in Blacksburg, Virginia

Since 2012, Amelia Tuckwiller, a self-admitted *Seinfeld* fan, has been co-organizing a Festivus celebration in Blacksburg, Virginia.

With a group of like-minded friends, now approaching twenty-five in number, they rent a room at PK's Bar & Grill in Blacksburg. Almost all of the celebrants are *Seinfeld* aficionados, though they often have a few non-*Seinfeld* fans and newcomers to the party. Some are even passersby who see the fun and want to join in.

For Amelia, the reason for celebrating Festivus is mostly a love of *Seinfeld* and a penchant for having fun. "I am a huge Seinfeld fan. I watch it every day to unwind," she readily admits. As for Festivus she adds, "I like that it is a secular holiday and anyone with a sense of humor can enjoy the nonsense of Festivus. It brings like-minded people together to have a good time."

They normally celebrate on the Saturday before Christmas. This works out best, as they are in a college town and it's

Full of Festivus spirit, sisters Amelia Tuckwiller (left) and Gloria Tuckwiller (right) gather around the Festivus pole.

better to wait until the students are away for holidays.

So, what is a Festivus party with Amelia like? Plenty of Fun!

First, they ask people to wear *Seinfeld* t-shirts. However, they also allow puffy shirts, 8-ball jackets, denim vests, manzieres or bros, Executive raincoats, European carryalls, or anything made of velvet.

There isn't an elaborate or expensive Festivus pole. It is a simple affair, made of two wrapping paper rolls taped together and covered in aluminum foil. It does the job and it didn't cost a penny!

As the guests arrive, they all don name tags... but not with their real name. They must pick a name from the "character board" which has the names of minor *Seinfeld* characters such as Todd Gack, Jackie Chiles, Babs, Delores, Mulva, Sidra, Bubble Boy, Bob Sacamano, etc.

The evening eventually proceeds to a round of *Seinfeld* trivia. They divide into teams and pick a non-*Seinfeld* fan to read the questions because, as Amelia puts it, "they legitimately have no idea what is going on!" They do keep score, but the winners don't get anything, other than the glory of victory.

Outside the trivia competition, there really aren't any Feats of Strength, though they might play-act a few rounds of arm wrestling just for a few pictures.

As for the Airing of Grievances, Amelia describes a fun procedure. "We pass around a shoe box for the Airing of Grievances. People fill out slips of paper and stuff the box throughout the night. At the end of the night, my sister usually reads them." Amelia adds, "Most of the grievances are about things that have happened over the course of the evening, for example 'Who is the new guy... who invited him?', 'What's the deal with Ovaltine?' and 'I just saw someone double-dip a chip!' It is always fun to try to guess who wrote what!"

It sure seems that *Seinfeld*-based fun is now an annual tradition in Blacksburg, VA. Will the fun endure? When asked if they plan to continue Festivus in the years to come, Amelia responded, "Yes, we plan to continue as long as we are able!"

Festivus in Kandahar, Afghanistan

Aulton White proudly reported that a Festivus celebration took place in December 2011, while he was deployed with the 82nd Airborne Division Headquarters at Kandahar, Afghanistan.

"With all the things going on in Afghanistan I felt there should be something to get away from all the hoopla and tradition and bring in a more secular celebration of Festivus," Aulton recounted.

Members of the HQ scrounged a Festivus pole from what they could find laying around, and once they erected the aluminum pole in a common area, people started placing their grievances on the pole.

They also established a snack room where they placed some appropriate food items to serve as a Festivus dinner. Then they setup a "Corn Hole" game (beanbag toss) and used it as their Feats of Strength.

"Even though the traditional pole is unadorned, we used it as a place to post our grievances using post-it notes,"

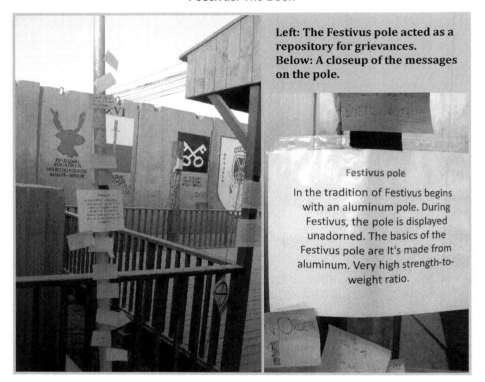

Left: The Festivus pole acted as a repository for grievances.
Below: A closeup of the messages on the pole.

Festivus pole

In the tradition of Festivus begins with an aluminum pole. During Festivus, the pole is displayed unadorned. The basics of the Festivus pole are It's made from aluminum. Very high strength-to-weight ratio.

Aulton explained. Since they continued to operate on a 24/7 basis throughout the holidays and had no days off, they continued to post their grievances on the pole as much as they could.

"We did put up our pole around the 20th of December," Aulton added. "All members of the HQ company of the 82nd Airborne Division were able to be a part of the Festivus Celebration if they so chose. As you can see many did post their grievances for all to see."

Finally, an FYI for all who are wondering about the grievance on the pole stating "Gen Order #1". Apparently, this is the order that made all types of drinking alcohol prohibited, including beer.

Happy Festivus from Heather and her family!

Dear Son: It's Your Heritage

For Heather S. from Columbus, Georgia, Festivus is a day she looks forward to during the holidays. When her family is able, they normally get together on the 23rd of December for Festivus.

For Heather's family, the first celebration of Festivus "just happened" one year when her step-son's girlfriend came to visit on the 23rd of December. Heather made a spur of the moment decision that it was time for the family to have Feats of Strength. Thus, an annual tradition began.

Festivus at Heather's usually begins with spaghetti or pizza dinner, followed by the Airing of Grievances and finally the Feats of Strength. The Festivus pole is a thrifty accessory, being that it is a simple three-foot closet rod that was leftover from a recent renovation. As for the grievances, Heather says they are usually light-hearted, such as, "I don't see you enough," or "you don't clean your room".

After dinner the Feats of Strength are held. "The first year we just did *Wii Sports*," Heather explained. "Then for a couple of years we battled each other in the *Just Dance* video game. The last Festivus celebration we played Putt-Putt

123

golf." It sounds like healthy family fun!

Heather likes that Festivus is not based on any religion. However, that's not the only reason she loves Festivus. Heather is a huge *Seinfeld* fan, and the Festivus episode is one of her favorites. She takes pride in the fact that she now has a reason to quote Frank Costanza. This past year, when her son questioned why he had to celebrate Festivus, Heather responded with, "It's your heritage."

A Festivus 5K for Autism

A road race in December can be spiced up with a Festivus theme, as the husband and wife team of Cindy and Rick Johnson of Salem, Massachusetts have discovered.

The third annual Festivus 5K took place on Sunday the 14th of December, 2014. The winner was Steve Gendron of Lowell, Massachusetts with a time of 16:45. The women's overall winner for the third year in a row was Katheryn Cooper of Marblehead, with a time of 19:04.

Usually about 400 runners participate. However, Cindy says, "We also have had virtual runners from around the world participate from countries such as Mozambique, Germany, Thailand, Paraguay, and Mali. Festivus is for the rest of us, so we work hard to accommodate everyone!"

More importantly, the 2014 race brought in $12,000. The funds, which went to the Doug Flutie Jr. Foundation for Autism, are destined for autism advocacy and care. The race was also hosted by Finz Seafood & Grill, co-organized by volunteers from the Parents United of Salem, and sponsored by many local businesses.

Consider first that this is not the "Human Fund". This is real money, real need and real charity; the focus of this race is such an extremely important matter. In fact, over its three year run, the race has brought in more than $30,000 for autism charities. Fantastic!

That being said, there is still lots of room for fun. The race does feature a tempting schmear of Festivus and *Seinfeld*-themed awards. The overall male and female winners receive a Festivus pole trophy and the top overall team wins "The Wiz" award. (Because nobody beats "The Wiz". Nobody.) In fact, the overall winner commented that the first-place desktop Festivus pole trophy was "the coolest trophy he'd ever gotten."

No soup for you! Robert Fournier of Salem, Massachusetts runs the race dressed as "The Soup Nazi".

"We are doing our part to help spread Festivus cheer!" Cindy exclaimed. "The first year had many people running because the race fit into their calendar, or Festivus-loving friends encouraged them to sign up. Now, everyone who runs knows what Festivus is all about."

There are also awards for best costume. Costumes must be holiday or *Seinfeld*-themed. "We've seen an increase in people who dress in *Seinfeld*-themed costumes participating in our contest. The grievances also get more and more creative each year," Cindy explained.

Runners are encouraged to air their grievances on race day, when they are asked to openly share their disappointment about something.   The best of the grievances are read aloud at a post-race gathering.

A few of the more creative grievances have been:

- Bathroom selfies.
- I have run the same 5K race for the last 2 years. I was beaten by the same Golden Retriever both times.
- Patrick Swayze did not win an Oscar for Road House.
- When a person starts a race early just because a car backfires.
- Why is Festivus for the rest of us? Why isn't it just for me?
- Winter makes my butt look big.
- There is no federal funding for Bigfoot research.
- My grievance is with runner 446 who never heard of Festivus and tried to cram over the Internet. I challenge him to Feats of Strength!

Katheryn Cooper, the Women's overall winner, proudly accepts her trophy, a mini-Festivus pole.

- Tights are not pants.

The Grievance Contest seems to be a successful addition to the event. "We have a lot of people participate in our grievance contest." Cindy explained. "As soon as people finish up running, they often look to see if their grievance was chosen as a winner before they check their race results. Our overall winner this year commented on how winning a case of Junior Mints as part of the Grievance contest was better than coming in first in the race itself!"

The Festivus pole is also a big hit. At the end of the

race, participants flock to the pole to take a picture. "We tried to have it engraved with the names of race winners," Cindy said. "But we've been told it is too hard to engrave an aluminum pole. It does have a high strength-to-weight ratio, you know."

Are you wondering if there are any Feats of Strength? Well, the race itself is a feat of strength, and as Cindy puts it, "the Feat of Strength comes from our 'Feet of Strength'."

If you look around online, you will discover that there are plenty of other Festivus themed road races around the world. They seem to be popping up in various places, with organizers taking advantage of the Festivus theme to add fun and excitement to the event. Look for one close to you, or if you are in the Salem area, check out Festivus5k.com. It looks like plenty-o-fun!

Lara and Steve's Wonderful Workplace Festivus

Is Wisconsin the epicenter of Festivus? It might be! Lara and Steve, co-workers in a local government office in Madison, Wisconsin, are prepared to keep the Festivus flame burning in the Badger State. They plan to continue hosting an annual office Festivus party for as long as they are able. That's commitment!

How long have they been celebrating Festivus at work? It is vague, Lara explains, "It started one year at work, the exact year is a matter of office lore and legend. The earliest reference is a calendar invitation for a Festivus lunch in 1999, but our memory is unclear as to what exactly happened that year. We also found an archived email from 2007 that references the bagel strike as having ended and that free bagels were available. In 2009, we found an invitation to a Festivus lunch."

2009 is the year that Lara and Steve turned an office tradition of bringing treats every day for the month of December into a "BLT" Festivus party. They augmented the

BLT sandwiches with a plain aluminum coat rack, which served as a Festivus pole.

"People had to serve themselves, it was very no frills, but it was a novelty to have fresh BLTs in the office," Lara said.

Keep in mind that the idea of "no stress" is exactly why they celebrate Festivus. "It is an antidote to the usual December holiday madness," Lara explains. "Festivus is supposed to be easy and stress-free."

Since 2009, they have continued Festivus as a yearly tradition. It is normally scheduled on a lunch hour as close to

Only a Wisconsin made pole will do for Lara and Steve. A Wagner Companies pole now finds itself as an object of strength and beauty at their annual Festivus party.

December 23 as possible. Coworkers from the office are invited. Sometimes a few other folks from the same floor show up. One year they even hosted the Mayor.

These days they have abandoned the BLTs for a potluck meal, serving only foods that have some reference to *Seinfeld*, such as bagels, black and white cookies, marble rye, Entenmann's, calzones, pretzels, big salad, frozen yogurt and Junior Mints.

"This year somebody brought shrimp... the ocean called," Lara said. "One year I brought a briefcase full of saltine crackers." (A reference to the episode "The Bizarro Jerry" (*S08E03*) where Kramer "works" at Brandt-Leland.)

That didn't go over very well, but I thought it was perfect as it is supposed to be a somber holiday." Did we mention "Festivus is a Somber Holiday" is how Lara sees the theme of Festivus? "But nobody else agrees," Lara laments.

They also have the Airing of Grievances and arm wrestling for the Feats of Strength. According to Lara, the Airing of Grievances is everyone's favorite part. "I put out paper forms for people to fill out throughout the morning, and they put them in a basket in the kitchen. During lunch we read them out loud and try to guess who wrote it or generally just have a good laugh."

In 2014, they voted on the best grievance and awarded boxes of "Soup Nazi" soup to the top two choices. Then, they posted the best grievances to the Festivus pole for people to admire throughout the day.

After the meal and the Airing of Grievances, they have the Feats of Strength. The yearly tradition is for the Office Manager, Sue, to arm wrestle Steve. Others are also invited to take part. "We do not force anyone to participate in Feats of Strength but if there was someone named George in our office we would insist that he fight his father," Lara adds.

Over the years, they've even improved the Festivus pole. "A few years ago my coworker Steve bought a real Festivus pole," Lara said. "He bought it from the Wisconsin Historical Museum, strangely enough. They had Festivus poles for sale in their gift shop. We made a special trip one year at lunchtime to buy one for our office Festivus party."

What? Festivus poles for sale in the gift shop. Maybe they should change Wisconsin's nickname from the "Badger State" to the "Festivus State".

Festivus in Hawthorne, New Jersey

Annually on December 23rd, Meaghan Tuohey hosts a Festivus party in her home. For the past ten years, nearly one hundred of her family, friends and co-workers have gathered at her home to celebrate the strange new holiday. It's a family friendly event as plenty of children are usually in attendance.

Happy Festivus

Let Festivus Commecicus

When: December 23, 2014, 7pm

Where: ███████████ Hawthorne

Bring: Dessert

Fine Print: Miss two Festivii and you are off the list,
which you don't want to happen because next year is the 10th Anniversary Festivus;
children and miscellaneous relatives are welcome;
no need to RSVP, surprise me but if you have questions: ███████████

Recipients of Meaghan's invitation are best advised to read the fine print!

Some celebrants are *Seinfeld* fans. They completely understand the theme. Meanwhile, many others have no idea what Festivus is, and they come for the party. Some years they have the episode running in a loop on a television screen, clearly to sate the appetite of the *Seinfeld* fanatics that are in attendance.

Using regular snail mail, Meaghan sends out humorous invitation cards in advance. According to Meaghan, one of the stipulations of the invitation process is, "If you miss two Festivii in a row, you are off the invite list. It's a rule guests take seriously. To maintain their spot on the list we have had people just run in for a few minutes or just send one spouse."

Festivus traditions remain an integral part of the celebration. Meaghan displays a traditional 6-foot aluminum pole and offers a grievance box to the guests, which they fill with gripes. "We air the grievances by reading them aloud at the end of the party," Meaghan confirms. Though she did add, "We forgo the feats of strength due to liability issues." This is likely a smart move... did we mention Meaghan is a lawyer?

One of the regular invitees has taken to saving each year's grievances and then returning the next year to post lasts year's notes somewhere in the house (usually the bathroom door).

The food at the party is potluck. Guests are assigned to bring either an appetizer or a dessert. The appetizers are served first. As soon as they are finished there is a "Parade of Desserts" where the desserts are revealed.

Is there music? Yes! However, it is Christmas music that is usually played throughout the party. It's not meant as an offense to Festivus, but more as a nod to the season.

This sounds like a fancy, fun shindig. Are you wondering what I'm wondering? How does a person get themselves on the invitee list in the first place?

Michelle Makes the Switch

No, we are not referring to the "Roommate Switch", a term made popular in *Seinfeld* episode "The Switch" (*S06E11*). We are referring to a switch to Festivus.

Michelle L., from Burbank, California, normally hosts a Christmas party for about twenty family members and friends during the weekend between Christmas and New Year's. However, in 2014 she decided to make it a "Festivus" party. Why would she do such a thing? It's rather simple, as she explained, "My father and I are huge *Seinfeld* fans!"

This is very clear when you see how Festivus at Michelle's place plays out... nearly every aspect of the party is *Seinfeld* themed, and clearly Michelle knows how to throw a party.

The food is entirely *Seinfeld* related. From the steaming crock pot of Mulligatawny soup (Kramer's favorite) to the marble rye bread, muffin tops, pizza bagels, black and white cookies, cinnamon babka, Junior Mints and Snickers bars (cut up into bite size pieces with a mini-plastic fork, of course).

Ain't she sweet! Michelle's daughter, Hannah, poses with the Festivus pole.

Was there a Festivus pole? Absolutely! The pole was fashioned by Michelle's father, the other *Seinfeld* fan in the family. It was a plain shower curtain rod purchased at Home Depot and held upright in a flower pot. "It worked out perfectly," Michelle added.

For fun they played *Seinfeld* Trivia,

Above: The game board for the "I'm Sorry. But the Answer is Moops" *Seinfeld* trivia game. (Fifteen questions with hidden answers)

Below Left: Can you spare a square? The *Seinfeld* gags are everywhere in the house!

Below Right: A bowlful of Pez party favors is offered to the guests.

133

which was appropriately named as the "I'm Sorry but the Answer is Moops Seinfeld Trivia Game". They also had a regift exchange. "People brought Christmas presents that they would like to regift," Michelle explained.

In decorating for Festivus, Michelle seems to have included as many *Seinfeld* references as she could. There is even a sign in the washroom above the toilet paper dispenser that says, "Can you spare a square?"

As parting gifts for the guests she offered Pez dispensers in a bowl decorated with a photo of Jerry Seinfeld taken from the *Seinfeld* episode "The Pez Dispenser" (*S03E14*).

When asked about the Feats of Strength, Michelle reported, "Did not do it this year. Maybe next year." Yes, it seems that Michelle has already decided to continue Festivus as a yearly tradition, and the planning has already begun. "Next year, the plan is to feature a make your own pizza station," she said.

We wonder if cucumber will be available as a pizza topping? Yum!

A Festivus Pole for Dillsburg, PA

In December 2014, Paul Tucker from Dillsburg, Pennsylvania started a new Festivus tradition.

"I became an atheist about six years ago. I started to have real problems with celebrating Christmas without believing in any of it," Paul explained. "All of my family are very religious and so we have all the Christmas displays in our homes. I thought the Festivus pole would be a light-hearted way to indicate that there was someone in the family with a different take on things."

But, why Festivus?

It's clearly because of Paul's love for *Seinfeld*. "I was a big fan of Seinfeld and thought the episode was fabulous," Paul added.

Paul usually puts up his Festivus pole at home along with a regular Christmas tree. However, in December 2014 he had a banner made and also put up a Festivus display in the Dillsburg town square.

Paul is a soft-spoken man, and he really doesn't want to insult anyone. "I wanted to counter the nativity scene that has been put up there for thirty plus years," Paul clarified. "Again, an attempt to let others know that there were people in the community that didn't believe exactly the same thing. So, it was kind of a challenge, but one that would hopefully bring a smile to one's face."

Paul reports that he has received dozens of positive remarks

It's a proper Festivus in Dillsburg now that Paul Tucker has placed a pole in the town square.

about the Festivus display at the town square, though he also adds that there have been a few negative remarks as well.

The Festivus pole Paul has at home is pretty impressive. "I have a 1.5-inch diameter 6-foot tall aircraft grade aluminum pole that I got at the Dillsburg Aeroplane Works. I paid around $40 for it," Paul described. It sounds like it has a very high strength-to-weight ratio!

Meanwhile, the pole at the town square was a 2-inch PVC pipe with shiny aluminum duct tape wrapped around it. "I didn't want to take the chance that someone would steal it for the aluminum, or use it to damage something," Paul explained.

We now know that Paul sets up two different Festivus poles, but does he also observe the Festivus tradition of the airing of grievances? "I guess putting up the Festivus display on the square is how I air my grievance with the town," Paul said. "My grievance is that they allow a religious display on town property."

Paul would rather say, "He observes Festivus rather than celebrates it." As for the Feats of Strength, Paul gets a pass. Paul's son has said he doesn't want to wrestle his father to the ground because he knows that his Dad has a bad back.

Happy Festivus Paul! Here's to many more in the coming years.

An Australian Festivus

Imagine this... people celebrating Festivus, outdoors, in January. They are in a beautiful park, basking in the warmth of the hot sun. Children are playing games, adults are drinking cold beverages and everyone is gorging themselves on BBQ. It's no dream if you live in Sydney, Australia.

Annually, between 2006 and 2012, members of the Sydney Atheists, Sydney Skeptics, and New South Wales Humanists would come together with their children and guests to celebrate Festivus in Jubilee Park. At its peak, well over 100 adults and children attended.

We can all understand the idea of getting together in a park for a

All paths lead to Festivus on a sunny January afternoon in Sydney, Australia.

picnic with like-minded individuals. But, why Festivus?

"Festivus exposed the rort that is Christmas," explained Steve Marton, President of the Sydney Atheists. "It was a hilarious concept."

The day was usually filled with Festivus-style fun. The group would set up a Festivus pole and establish a section where you could write down grievances and hang them up, while the most outspoken of the group would just stand next to the pole and air their grievances verbally for everyone to enjoy.

Feats of strength were held, which usually consisted of light family-fun competitions such as sack races, a tug of war or an obstacle course. There was even a competition where clocks were tossed like Frisbees. Why? For fun!

Unfortunately, the tradition ended after Festivus 2012, as the rules for booking public parks in Sydney changed, leaving at least one grievance remaining unaired. A grievance against the Sydney parks administration, maybe?

Top: Down under in Sydney, they're making time fly! You just toss the clock as far as you can. Why? Because it's fun! (That's all you need to know...)
Bottom: In Sydney, the outspoken stand in a shady spot next to the pole and tell everyone what's been bothering them... then they eat BBQ. How cathartic!

Festivus at Little Jerry's

Festivus does not come and go without being honored at Little Jerry's, a *Seinfeld*-themed restaurant in Tacoma, Washington. In December 2012, the staff and several devoted customers celebrated their first ever Festivus, including an "Airing of Grievances" outside in the parking lot.

Owner Anthony Valadez has been a *Seinfeld* fan since he saw the show in its first run. As a result, the restaurant is decorated with every piece of *Seinfeld* memorabilia you can imagine, including a large portrait of Kramer. A

Is Tara Valadez on strike? No! She's just having fun at Festivus.

television above the main dining area plays *Seinfeld* episodes.

The menu items are also *Seinfeld* themed. For example, the "Pigman" is a BLT sandwich. There are other aptly named dishes such as the "Shrinkage", a breakfast special that features mini-sausages on the side.

When December arrives, the staff pull the Festivus pole from the crawlspace. Guests are then invited to write their grievances on post-it notes and place them on the pole.

A *Seinfeld* based restaurant is the best place in the world to celebrate Festivus. If you ever find yourself in or near Tacoma at Festivus-time, check it out. You could have breakfast surrounded by Seinfeldism, or at least attempt to discover if Little Jerry can really run from here to Newman's in under thirty seconds.

Top left and right: The grievances on Little Jerry's pole range from a mean wife and an expensive vet to cell phone use at lunch and the lack of a frogger machine. Below: You'll find this unique *Seinfeld* Scrabble board on the wall at Little Jerry's.

Festivus in Philly

Where is the best place to celebrate Festivus in Philadelphia? In a pub, of course!

Since 2012, Festivus has been celebrated at the Grey Lodge Public House in Northeast Philadelphia. Usually held on the Sunday before Christmas, the idea to host Festivus originated with the Grey Lodge proprietor, Mike Scotese, better known as "Scoats".

Unique to Grey Lodge is the "Holding the Big Mug O'Pennies" feat of strength. "People hold the Big Mug O'Pennies out at arm's length and we time them,"

The historic Grey Lodge Pub, 6235 Frankford Avenue in Northeast Philadelphia

Scoats explained. "Their time is announced. It becomes a real competition as people try to outdo each other."

Apparently, it is not an easy achievement. Even the strongest participants have struggled badly, quickly rolling their arm or eventually just falling over. There are separate divisions for men and women. Spilling the pennies causes the timer to stop, and when the person looks like they are ready to lose it, someone standing by grabs the pennies before the change hits the floor.

Aside from the Big Mug O'Pennies, patrons are encouraged to demonstrate their own feat of strength. In fact, two years in a row, Andrew Jardel proved his ability to balance a stool on his chin.

Does anyone air his or her grievances? "Yes, we have a

microphone set up," Scoats said. "People get up occasionally and air their grievances. Usually, as more Christmas beers are drank, participation increases."

Aside from the Festivus-related fun, the pub hosts a round of *Seinfeld* Trivia with prizes, as well as a "Twisted Holiday Songs Sing Along", featuring a slate of holiday parody songs such as "Frothy the Snowman", "I Saw Daddy Punching Santa Claus" and "Truly Rotten Christmas". This is followed by an ugly sweater contest, with prizes awarded for best ugly sweater, nicest ugly sweater, and best homemade ugly sweater. The prize categories seem vague, but the fun is guaranteed.

When people start celebrating Festivus, miracles begin to occur...

When asked if they had a Festivus pole, Scoats explained, "Turns out we have two. I bought the first one from Lowes (the good one). It brought back childhood memories of shopping for a Christmas tree with my family. The next year when I checked the basement rafters to make sure our pole was still there, I saw there were two up there. It was a Festivus Miracle!"

Will they host Festivus in the coming years? "Definitely," Scoats

Art McKee pits his strength against the Big Mug O'Pennies.

confirmed. "It became a classic Grey Lodge event the first year we did it."

Lastly, it wouldn't be a Grey Lodge Pub event without great beer. The pub always carries a nice selection of Christmas seasonals, ready for Festivus libation. If you're in Philly, what's stopping you from joining in, grabbing a beer, and attempting to hoist a heavy mug of loose change?

A Saskatchewan Festivus

Annually since 2013, a group of like-minded individuals have met in Regina, Saskatchewan to celebrate Festivus.

For those who may be unaware, Regina, a growing city with a population of about a quarter-million people, is located smack-dab in the middle of the Canadian prairies. Famous for the warmth of its citizens, it is also well known for frigid winter temperatures.

Billed as "Festivus, A Holiday for the Rest of Us", the event is sponsored by the Regina chapter of the "Centre for Inquiry", an organization made up of agnostics, apostates, atheists, freethinkers, naturalists, pastafarians, rationalists, scientific pantheists, secular humanists, skeptics, or related whathaveyouists... literally the "rest of us".

"We have done it since 2013, and plan to continue hosting it annually," said Diane McLean, Branch Manager for CFI Regina. "Our Festivus celebration is typically held in the first week or two of December, rather than on the actual Festivus date of December 23rd. We do this because people's schedules are typically less crowded at the start of December, allowing more to attend."

The event has grown since its inauguration. In the first year, they filled a room that could seat approximately twenty-five attendees. In the second year, they booked additional space, filling a section of the restaurant that seats about fifty.

The location of the celebration, Beer Bros. Gastropub & Deli, provides a top-notch three-course meal combined with

Soaring into a spectacular Saskatchewan sunset, the Flying Spaghetti Monster, chief symbol of Pastafarianism, is guided by a shiny Festivus pole.

optional beer pairings, making for an excellent Festivus feast. The food and beer sounds decent enough to make any evening complete. But, what about the usual trappings of Festivus?

"We always erect a Festivus pole. It's an aluminum pole that remains undecorated in defiance of the consumerism and tradition of the other winter holidays," Diane explained. "We also have Feats of Strength, which involves challenging each other to arm wrestling contests or thumb wars."

"Airing of Grievances usually occurs before the meal," Diane said. "Anyone can talk about grievances they have against others. This is a chance for friends to poke fun at each other, or for more serious grievances to be aired about current events, politicians, etc."

The party also includes a voluntary white elephant gift exchange, where participants are invited to provide a gift worth $20 or less. The gifts are placed around the Festivus pole until dinner is complete, then the exchange begins.

"The gifts are typically along the nerdy, creative, secular, or religious parody vein, some of which are homemade," Diane explained. "Examples of gifts have been shirts featuring references to Star Trek or Carl Sagan, paintings of the Flying Spaghetti Monster, various Star Wars propaganda, a custom made cutting board, a Jesus bobble head figurine (that seems to be regifted every year), and more!"

To lend some gravitas to the event, the organizers suggest the attendees wear semi-formal attire. "It gives people an excuse to air out their fancy digs and act pompous," Diane explained. "Besides, what's more fun than thumb wars in a suit, or poking fun at friends in sparkly heels?"

In Regina, one of the gifts placed under the Festivus pole was a paper sack containing what could only be imagined as cuddly creatures from the movie *Gremlins*. (It's actually a sack of nickels.)

Dry heave set to music Beefarino

Get Out

Close talker **Newman** Urban Sombrero

That's gold **Man hands** Jimmy legs

Nobody beats me because I'm The Wiz

Shrinkage

Happy Pappy **Serenity now** Jimmy's down

You gotta see the baby

Seinfeldism

Poppie's a little sloppy **The jerk store** Ribbon Bully

Oh the humanity Maybe the dingo ate your baby Double dip

Fugitive sex Baldist Queen of the castle Sideler

Schmoopie **Low talker** Oh Moses smell the rose

Hellooo La La La **Yada yada yada** Toe thumbs

Hipster doofus Vile weed

Shiksappeal

Coffee Table Book About Coffee Tables

Cartwright **Master of your domain** Giddyup

Re-gifter

Mimbo **Mulva Puffy shirt** You magnificent bastard

Yo Yo Ma Bad breaker-upper

These pretzels are making me thirsty

Yama hama I don't wanna be a pirate Pretty big matzah ball

High talker **No soup for you** I am aware

Two-face

I was in the pool **Marble rye** Cantstandya

Sweet Fancy Moses That's a shame

The move Soup Nazi Anti-dentite

The tap They're real and they're spectacular

Hello Newman Top of the muffin to you Moops

Big salad **Bubble boy** Sexual camel

In the vault

Spongeworthy

You can stuff your sorries in a sack

Not that there's anything wrong with that

1st and 1st You are so good looking Kavorka

Manssiere/Bro Conjugal visit sex

Chapter 16 : What's the Deal With Seinfeldism?

If there was a religion associated with Festivus it might be called Seinfeldism.

> **Seinfeldism**: 1. A catchphrase that's been used on the TV show Seinfeld. 2. A demonstration of an inordinate love for the television series Seinfeld.

> **Seinfeldist**: Someone who practices Seinfeldism.

When someone is a Seinfeldist you'll know it. They overtly demonstrate an unusual knowledge of every *Seinfeld* joke, gag, character and episode. They can relate any ordinary event to something that happened on *Seinfeld*, and then laugh about it. They are often solitary, but when they form up in packs of three or more, watch out! They begin to monopolize every social moment with their inane banter about *Seinfeld*. If you're a Seinfeldist, this is a wonderful moment; if you are not, then you will be confused and likely bored to tears.

Seinfeldism is fandom to the level of Dudeism, a philosophy and lifestyle inspired by the film *The Big Lebowski*, or Bronyism, a cult-like love of *My Little Pony*.

Seinfeld started as a "water cooler show", which meant people talked about the episodes the day after they aired. It created a buzz, especially around the catchphrases that it precipitated, such as "yada yada yada", "close-talker" and "master of your domain". *Seinfeld* was unsurpassed in its stealthy method of infiltrating popular culture. No other television show had ever become a part of people's daily life

There is nothing more "Seinfeldian" than Tom's Restaurant in the Morningside Heights neighborhood of Manhattan.

in such a remarkable way.

Seinfeld was wildly popular in its day, and it seems to have retained its cachet, even seventeen years after it went off the air. While this is largely due to the continued availability of re-runs on television, there is clearly something else happening.

In its day, *Seinfeld* was ground-breaking. Critics and fans alike agreed that nothing like it had ever aired on television before, which definitely fed its popularity. Now, a quarter century after it first aired, it's seen as the show that changed everything. To its ever faithful fans, *Seinfeld* is still seen as funny and relevant. The comedy holds up. Long live *Seinfeld*!

Aren't Festivus People Just Seinfeld People?

Haven't you noticed how so many of the Festivus celebrations we've seen have included more than just Festivus traditions? Typically, there are plenty of other *Seinfeld* references included as a part of the party.

In our 2014 FestivusWeb.com user survey, we asked our readers four questions about *Seinfeld*. These questions were designed to

Seinfeldism Test

1. **Which actor/actress NEVER guest starred in the Seinfeld series?**
   a. Amanda Peet
   b. Teri Hatcher
   c. Bryan Cranston
   d. Judge Reinhold
   e. Robert Stack

2. **Which of these situations NEVER occurred in the Seinfeld series?**
   a. Newman infests Jerry's apartment with fleas
   b. Elaine dated an anti-abortionist
   c. Kramer makes money by selling home-made pizza pies
   d. Jerry gets sick after eating a cookie
   e. George pretends to be a marine biologist

3. **Which of these phrases/statements is NOT a common Seinfeldism?**
   a. Yo Yo Ma
   b. I don't want to be a pirate!
   c. I was in the pool!
   d. Café au lait
   e. Yada Yada Yada

4. **Which does NOT describe a plot line seen in a Seinfeld episode?**
   a. Jerry shaves his chest
   b. The Costanzas move to Florida
   c. Kramer is afraid of clowns
   d. Elaine dates a rabbi
   e. George eats food from the garbage

gauge the respondents' *Seinfeld* acumen. The goal was to prove how people who celebrate Festivus are also serious *Seinfeld* fans.

The questions were tricky; this was done on purpose. Many people love *Seinfeld*, but only a real fan would be able to answer all four questions correctly. In addition, you really couldn't guess the answers. Either you knew the answer, or you didn't.

The average overall score among all users who celebrate Festivus was 55.2%. A small portion of the respondents, 18%, scored a perfect 100%, representing hard-core *Seinfeld* fans. Incidentally, respondents had the best success on Question #4 with an average score of about 68%.

What does this mean? Approximately half of the people who celebrate Festivus are Seinfeldists! How scientific was this? ...not very. Right now the Seinfeldists are saying, "Tell me more Mr. Science", while the non-Seinfeldists are shrugging their shoulders and saying, "Tell me something I didn't know."

How did you do in the short quiz? ...

Correct answers: 1(e), 2(c), 3(d), 4(d)

4/4: Expert Seinfeldist   3/4: Professional Seinfeldist

2/4: Amateur Seinfeldist   1/4: Lucky guesser

0/4: What's a Seinfeld?

Let's all go to Seinfeld Night at... (Fill in the blank)!

With Seinfeldism still being strong in our society, "Seinfeld Night" has become one of the most popular types of promotions for sports teams, bars, clubs etc. We have three great examples for you, two from American sports teams who are attempting to attract paying customers to the turnstiles and one from a performance venue in Toronto, Canada. Enjoy the fun!

Brooklyn Cyclones Seinfeld Night

On 5 July 2014, at their Coney Island field, the Brooklyn Cyclones hosted a *Seinfeld* tribute night to honor the show's 25th

It's Seinfeld Night at Coney Island. Game day giveaway was a Keith Hernandez "Magic Loogie" Bobblehead.

anniversary. It turned out to be one of the most successful promotions they ever held, and prompted them to schedule a second Seinfeld Night to be held in the 2015 season.

Here are some of the *Seinfeld*-related nuances they incorporated into their game-day product:

- The players all warmed up in puffy shirts.
- The game day giveaway was a Keith Hernandez "Magic Loogie" Bobblehead Doll.
- The real Kenny Kramer was in attendance.
- Larry Thomas, the actor who played the "Soup Nazi" was also in attendance.
- George Costanza "Biggest Wallet" Contest.
- Marble rye fishing contest.
- Junior Mints toss.
- Elaine dancing contest. (All kicks and thumbs)
- Cereal eating contest.
- A competition to eat a candy bar with a fork.

Apparently there were plenty of "face painters" in attendance (you gotta support the team) and *Risk* (The Game of World Domination) was being played in the concourse. We hope nobody dared to try and take the Ukraine.

Incidentally, the 2015 version of Seinfeld Night has been dubbed the "Summer of George". Plans include Kramer-inspired "Technicolor Dreamcoat" uniforms (they are breathtaking) as well as on-field events such as a Costanza Trash Eating Competition, an Ovaltine Drinking Relay and an Urban Sombrero Catch. Ole!

Seinfeld Night in Bakersfield

In honor of the 25th Anniversary of the first *Seinfeld* episode, the Bakersfield Condors, owned by the NHL's Edmonton Oilers, held a Seinfeld Night on 16 November 2014.

The players all wore special "Puffy" Jerseys for the game. To top that off, instead of their own names on the jerseys they had the names of *Seinfeld* characters: Jerry, George, Kramer, Newman, Frank Costanza, Puddy, J. Peterman, Steinbrenner, Morty Seinfeld, Uncle Leo, Art Vandelay, Kenny Bania, Lloyd Braun, Jackie Chiles, Crazy Joe Davola, Mandelbaum, Bubble Boy, Keith Hernandez, Mickey Abbott and Assman,

The goalie was given the name "The Wiz", because we all know "nobody beats The Wiz".

Also, the jerseys featured the names of sponsors, which were all *Seinfeld* related: Vandelay Industries, Pendant Publishing, Kramerica, Del Boca Vista, and plainly just "RESTAURANT", a reference to Monk's Café which had a similarly named sign seen in nearly every *Seinfeld* episode.

Other *Seinfeld* related gimmicks and promotions included an Elaine-style dance off and a rickshaw race around the ice. In the weeks after the game, the jerseys were auctioned off for charity, with surprising success.

It seems that *Seinfeld* lives on, and not just in syndicated reruns. It has clearly found new life in the realm of sports team promotions.

In a tribute to *Seinfeld*, the Bakersfield Condors wore "Puffy Shirt" jerseys, complete with *Seinfeld* related names and sponsors.

What's a Seinfeld Night Without Costumes?

On 8 February 2015, "Double Double Land", a performance venue located in Toronto, Canada's multicultural Kensington Market, hosted "Scenefeld: The Celebration". Billed as the *Seinfeld* costume-and-trivia party to end all *Seinfeld* costume-and-trivia parties, the sold-out evening featured approximately one hundred guests, all in costume.

There were plenty of puffy shirts, bras worn as a top and Elaine look-alikes in the crowd. As well as costumed fun, the party featured an elimination style *Scene It: Seinfeld* trivia tournament, *Seinfeld*-themed food, and live slap bass, a la the *Seinfeld* theme. The costume competition and the Elaine-style dance contest were both decided by applause.

At the end of the night, three audience-selected *Seinfeld* episodes were screened. There was also a screening of *Nothing*, an online mashup video which features every shot from *Seinfeld* where nothing happens.

That's right. A video about nothing, shown at a party celebrating a show about nothing. Makes perfect sense.

What's the Deal with the Seinfeld Apartment?

In our quest to prove the ongoing popularity of *Seinfeld*, we saved the best for last. An event so mind-blowing, heads were spinning like a top. Here it is... someone actually created a reproduction of the *Seinfeld* apartment!

To promote their release of the *Seinfeld* catalogue of reruns, *Hulu* produced a pop-up installation of the "Seinfeld Apartment". Located at the Manhattan based Milk Studios, 451 West 14th Street, from 24-28 June 2015, *Seinfeld* fans were able to tour a perfect replica of Jerry's Upper West Side apartment.

Visitors came in droves. To gain admittance to the free exhibit, it was reported fans waited over five hours in a lineup that stretched around the block... and then around a second street as well.[42]

As visitors approached the door to the apartment exhibit, security staff offered a chance to do a Kramer style entrance. Many individuals took them up on the offer, with plenty of photos and videos of inspired guests attempting to emulate Kramer reaching social-networking in great abundance, including one video taken on the first day of operation where an extremely enthusiastic visitor managed to break the door.

Once inside, fans were able to bask in the opulence of a perfectly maintained blue/gray couch, an impeccable kitchen with cereal boxes crowding the shelves, a familiar looking entertainment system, a bike on the wall and an old Macintosh computer in the far corner. When *Seinfeld* aired we never saw Jerry Seinfeld use the Mac or the bike. Apparently, he's still not using them, as they

The exterior of Jerry's apartment as shown in the series. The building is actually located at 757 S. New Hampshire Avenue, in the Koreatown neighborhood of Los Angeles, California. In this early morning shot, note the shadow of a Mexican fan palm from across the street.

were freely available for the exhibit.

The *Hulu* promotions team seems to have focussed on details. From the neatness of the entire set, to the magazines and cereal boxes placed in the proper location . Even the sink in Jerry's washroom was a perfect replica of the one we saw on *Seinfeld*. As Maraithe Thomas reported in *The Guardian*: "It really just feels like you're there, and that George or Elaine could rush in at any moment to say: 'You will not believe what just happened.'"[43]

Collocated with the apartment was a "Seinfeld Museum" with plenty of *Seinfeld* props on display. Visitors could gaze at a bottle of Bosco from "The Secret Code" *(S07E07)* or giggle at the sight of David Puddy's New Jersey Devils jersey from "The Face Painter" *(S06E23)*. There were plenty of other artifacts such as a Superman action figure, a well-worn copy of *Tropic of Cancer*, a Frogger machine, and of course, a Festivus pole.

So much of *Seinfeld* was on display... there was even a cracked egg surrounded by juice glasses and caution tape. Only a *Seinfeld* fan would understand a gag like this. So much giggling must have been heard.

As if that wasn't enough, also on display was a replica of the iconic booth from "Monk's Café" and the day couch where Kramer photographed a half-nude George Costanza. Fans were invited to use the couch for their own re-enactment of the photo, and many did. Some even removed their clothes down to their skivvies in an effort to fully mimic George Costanza. Why not? When would this opportunity ever reoccur?

The popularity of this exhibit seems to have been truly breathtaking. It makes one wonder if a more permanent museum is just around the corner.

In conclusion, we can see how the ongoing popularity of *Seinfeld* is entirely on display. It has been reported *Hulu* paid a whopping $180 million for the *Seinfeld* rights, and that's not chump change. They must think it was a good investment, clearly indicating *Seinfeld* retains a certain amount of cachet in the entertainment industry. There you have it!

On 18 November 2004, in a ceremony broadcasted on *C-SPAN*, Jerry Seinfeld donated his iconic puffy shirt to the Smithsonian's National Museum of American History. If you are planning a trip to Washington, D.C. you have the chance to see the "pirate" shirt on display alongside many other important national treasures.

Chapter 17 : The War on Festivus

Every year, the "War on Festivus" seems to get more bitter. What is this war, you ask? Sit back, and let us tell you a little tale of war.

First, the term "War on Festivus" is usually uttered in reference to the similarly phrased "War on Christmas", an expression which has been used (mostly in the media) to describe the outrage people have when they perceive the removal of the religious aspects of Christmas. You've probably witnessed this conflict being waged, especially in social media. We've all seen people expressing their outrage at being greeted with "Happy Holidays" instead of "Merry Christmas". In this war, bloodshed is replaced by outrage, and wounds are replaced by angry red faces. Unfortunately, it's mostly hyperbole.

The War on Festivus actually began when the *Seinfeld* Festivus episode aired in December 1997. Contained in that episode was the notion that the Costanza family had given up the religious aspects of Christmas and converted to a non-secular, made-up holiday named Festivus. Most people laughed, and nodded their heads in agreement. They saw the truth in Frank Costanza's hilarious explanation of going doll-shopping for his son, and finding Christmas had gotten too commercial, causing him to search for a "better way".

Most people, Christians and non-Christians alike, agreed that Frank was on to something. We all knew what Frank was referring to when he brought it up on *Seinfeld*. Christmas had indeed become too commercial! However, the vague notion of giving up on Christmas didn't resonate well for some Christians. For a narrow portion, Festivus was branded as an anti-Christian holiday.

Whether anti-Christian or not, people have been erecting Festivus poles in public places for some time. In 2007, a Wisconsin man received permission to erect a Festivus pole next to Green Bay City Hall's nativity scene. As well, in 2008 and 2009, a Festivus pole was placed in the rotunda of the Capitol building located in Springfield, Illinois. For the most part, these "erections" were received with the same light-hearted attitude in which they were intended.

The Battle of Utica

In December 2014, a "Happy Birthday Jesus we love you" sign was placed outside a Utica, New York fire station, causing immediate controversy and making national headlines.

On the 23rd of December, a small group of citizens decided to meet outside the fire station to celebrate Festivus. Wearing Festivus t-shirts and sporting signs with slogans such as "A Festivus for the Restivus", the well-behaved group of Festivus celebrants gathered to foster a climate of inclusion and respect for all people in the community.

"I gotta tell you, I haven't figured them out yet," Fire Chief Russell Brooks said as he gazed at the crooked Festivus pole made out of Utica Club beer cans. Meanwhile, he didn't attempt to ban the odd-looking pole; he insisted, however, that it be placed away from the "Happy Birthday Jesus" sign.

"A Festivus for the rest of us, we came today with our Festivus pole to celebrate our faith as well, we want the display at the fire department to reflect the diverse community we have in Utica," said Festivus celebrator Amy Francisco-Nugent to the local media.[44]

Thus, the battle ended with zero bloodshed. Indignation was replaced with a healthy discussion and sprinkled with a dose of good humor.

A "PBR" Festivus Pole

In December 2013, a Festivus pole made of Pabst Blue Ribbon beer cans was about to be placed in the Florida Capitol when a significant cannon shot was fired in the "War on Festivus". The reason behind this placement was to take advantage of the fact that the government would allow any special interest group to contribute a public display of any type. The "PBR" Festivus pole was specifically placed to protest the annual tradition of placing a nativity scene in the same location.

It's all too clear that once governments open up a space to be used by the public for religious displays, they can't begin to dictate what people will place there. They have to provide equal opportunity for all religions, thus granting the opportunity for anyone to erect anything. This has been done before. Festivus poles have been placed in public places in the past, and often next to nativity scenes. Often it is seen as an attempt to be humorous.

> "To me religious neutrality, which the government must adhere to, doesn't mean being secular. It means inviting people to the conversation, to bring all of themselves to the conversation, including their faith."[45]
>
> *Naheed Nenshi*
> *Mayor of Calgary, Alberta*

However, this particular display was considered antagonistic because it was constructed solely of beer cans! Additionally, the person who had arranged the placement was well-known local atheist, Chaz Stevens. Once the pole placement was approved, Stevens went even further by distributing a press release announcing his "victory". What he really wanted to do was to stir the pot, so to speak, and stir it he did. Once media outlets were reporting the story, Christians, especially far right-wing Christians and *Fox News*, began to take offense.

Just as quickly as you can imagine, some *Fox News*

personalities started to spin like a top. On a *Fox News* panel, correspondent Gretchen Carlson carped, "I am so outraged about this. Why do I have to drive around with my kids to look for Nativity scenes and be like, oh yeah kids look there's baby Jesus behind the Festivus pole made out of beer cans. It's nuts!"[46]

In a response to the *Fox News* outrage, *Mother Jones* magazine released an article with a quote from *Seinfeld* writer Dan O'Keefe: "Both displays have equal right to be there," he said. "But, you know, the *Fox News* outrage machine kicked into high gear, and I'm sure there were some hair-sprayed talking heads bobbing up and down, being outraged about it."[47]

Clearly, the *Fox News* indignation shows how the right-wing feels about anything that stands against Christian symbols. Is the outrage warranted? It certainly depends on your point of view; we will just leave it at that.

Thus, the war on Festivus was heightened. Soon after, on his popular nighttime faux-news program, Stephen Colbert weighed in on the story with, "In the guise of fighting a war to defend Christmas, they are actually going on the offensive in their war on Festivus."[48]

This seems to be a lot of something over nothing. Let's take stock of where we are... an atheist decided to stir up outrage from right-wing Christians; he was successful. The outrage rises. Meanwhile he smiles for the reporters as he admires his beer can Festivus pole. Then, Festivus is berated.

It takes two sides to fight a war. Unfortunately, Festivus is the innocent victim in this conflict. Frankly, they should have just left Festivus out of it. In the Florida case, the antagonist chose a Festivus pole because it is normally considered an outrageous symbol. Then in placing the pole next to a religious symbol he is implying the pole is on an equal level. Seen by some as hilarious, this act is also see by others as blasphemous. In this case, the Festivus pole is being used as a wedge, and, as far as we can tell, the pole wasn't chosen for any sort of passion for *Seinfeld* or Festivus itself.

It's good to know that not everybody fell for this, as the reaction from the folks who actually put up the Nativity scene in the Florida Capitol was much more measured.[49] In essence, they didn't care. They were happy to ignore the PBR Festivus pole, and just went on celebrating Christmas as they normally did. Reasonable people seem to be able to adopt a "live and let live" attitude, which usually results in contentment rather than disgruntlement.

Coincidentally, Larry O'Keefe, the middle son of Daniel O'Keefe Sr., has said that his father was a Pabst Blue Ribbon fan. "I think they must have done research," Larry said. "Because my dad's drink of choice was PBR... and he drank a lot of it! He was one of their biggest customers. In fact, to this day, when I smell it, I have to leave the room."[50]

The next time you smell old stale beer cans, think about that PBR Festivus pole, and remember how religious outrage can be a cause of much strife.

Is Festivus an Affront to Christianity?

It is true that Festivus is considered a secular-celebration, in that it is not allied with or against any particular religion. In fact, the *Seinfeld* Festivus episode contains very little reference to any anti-religion aspect of Festivus. Mind you, there is a small part of the script where Jerry mentions the "religious aspects of Christmas", but this element never plays out in the story. In fact, it is the commercialism of the holiday season which the *Seinfeld* Festivus story rails against.

In the *Seinfeld* world, the Costanza family has no clear religious affiliation. Is this a mistake? Not really... it likely never came up in any of the writer's meetings, the place where the entire *Seinfeld* universe was contrived. Even in the episode where George endeavors to convert to "Latvian Orthodox" in a hilarious attempt to impress a woman ("The Conversion" *S05E11*), there is no mention of the religion from which he was converting. It just wasn't important to the plot!

In the Festivus episode, there isn't any impression that it is replacing another religious celebration for the Costanzas. To Frank Costanza, Festivus is simply a way to express derision toward a society that has become self-centered and commercialized. For example, with Festivus you don't buy a tree, you simply erect a plain aluminum pole. You don't exchange gifts, you exchange complaints (grievances). Then, to complete the wacky trifecta, you finish the evening by wrestling the head of the household until he or she is pinned into submission.

Additionally, the "Real Festivus" as celebrated by the O'Keefe family was never meant to replace Christmas, as Larry O'Keefe has revealed. "My dad never actually said he wanted to replace Christmas, but he was heard to say how much he hated Christmas because it was Christian oppression."[51] Daniel O'Keefe Sr. certainly had his opinions. However, his views were usually kept to himself, and never meant to be antagonistic.

Clearly, no matter how you look at it, Festivus is not about religion... unless of course, you consider "Seinfeldism" a religion. Ironically, to many it is, and it is the very thing that fuels Festivus! *Seinfeld* finished its run on network television seventeen years ago, and it is still popular. Fueled largely by reruns, you may still hear references to "Yada Yada Yada", the cries of "Serenity Now", and the moan of "I don't want to be a Pirate!" *Seinfeld* is ingrained in our consciousness, and Festivus helps us celebrate the show so many have come to love.

Seinfeld helps us laugh, and Festivus has become the "holiday" where "Seinfeldism" is practiced. So, laugh away Festivusites! Enjoy your celebrations as they should be enjoyed, with *Seinfeld*-based mirth and merriment. When your regular holiday celebration arrives, whether you are Christian, Jew, Hindu, Buddhist, Muslim, Pagan, Atheist, Satanist... whateverist... choose to enjoy that as well. It's up to you.

Chapter 18 : Conclusion

The only remaining mystery of Festivus we haven't discussed is, "will Festivus last?"

The best answer is "possibly", since there's always going to be a desire for a different sort of holiday. For some people, a celebration that is centered on people instead of religion (or anything else) will always be desired. Festivus provided us with this notion... the idea of a celebration for the rest of us. We think the concept of such a holiday will have long lasting appeal, even though the specific idea of Festivus may well fade.

Today, the *Seinfeld* version of Festivus has momentum, mainly because of the frequency of the *Seinfeld* reruns that continue to entertain us on television and through popular culture references. However, *Seinfeld* reruns won't be on television forever. Some people might be upset by this revelation, but this certainty is inevitable. We know that everything eventually fades. For example, consider one of the most popular television shows six decades ago, *I Love Lucy*. For all its popularity back in the day, and despite its quality as a television show, it hasn't retained its popularity. Still, the lasting power of *Seinfeld* seems unprecedented. *Seinfeld* may eventually go the same route, but it may take a little longer.

When *Seinfeld* fades, will Festivus remain? Possibly, but likely only in the form that Daniel O'Keefe Sr. envisioned, and keeping with the original meaning of Festivus. We know there will always be a need for people to celebrate the holidays in a way that is unencumbered by social and religious constructs. Festivus is a hit today, and it will continue to be a hit, especially among future secularists. Mind you, in the future, the Festivus dish might be "Soylent Orange", people might be regifting "orgasmatrons", and the grievances will be against corporations that block the sky and make mankind pay for sunshine. Always remember, the original intended meaning of Festivus is to "do what you want" and not to do what others tell you to do. Plenty of people will continue to embrace this idea in the years to come.

In the spirit of Daniel O'Keefe's creation, we should all have the holiday that gives us meaning, freedom and pleasure. It's the holiday for the rest of us; let's all enjoy Festivus in the way it was intended, and keep on enjoying it for decades to come.

In closing, when Dan O'Keefe Jr., was asked if he believes Festivus will continue, even after Seinfeld reruns go off the air, he responded, "Hey, the hair and toenails continue to grow even after death, right?"

There you have it. Festivus forever!

Afterword

I have a large family, and we have always celebrated Christmas together. It's just the way it has been done for as long as I can recall. However, in December 2005, our tradition took a turn, as our mother was sick in the hospital over the Christmas holidays. Suddenly, our regular Christmas plans had to be put on hold. After all, how could we celebrate Christmas together when we needed to be by Mom's side at the hospital?

It was around 23 December 2005 when my younger sister Renee declared that we should all go to her place and have a quick "Festivus Party". Since she lived very close to the hospital, this seemed okay. The food was potluck style, and everybody brought what he or she could. We never had time for shopping, so we just found whatever old unwanted item we had and brought it to the gathering as a "regift", as per Renee's instructions. The party worked out for the best. We were able to blow off some steam at a stressful time, and still be nearby for Mom. A little while after Christmas, Mom recovered... and a year later we decided to celebrate Festivus again... and again the year after. Festivus has been an annual event during my family's holiday season since 2005.

In our family, we still celebrate Christmas as we normally did in the past. In fact, Christmas remains the most important family gathering of the year. Festivus just adds to the family fun, and gives us another excuse to get together as a family. Why not? We still like each other, we all enjoy food and drink, we still have plenty of old crap to regift, and we still love *Seinfeld*... Festivus is fun and, combined with the fact that most of us are *Seinfeld* fans, it's a winning combination. Festivus allows an opportunity for members of my family to

Is that one-eyed clown giving you the heebie-jeebies? Regift it at Festivus. Someone in my family did.

get together and joke about all things *Seinfeld*. The holiday is low-key, especially when compared to Christmas, and it is surprisingly easy to celebrate.

Every year our Festivus changes slightly, however we usually have a potluck and we regularly regift old crap from the past. In fact, the regifting has become one of the favorite elements of our Festivus.

Back when we started, we never even had a Festivus pole. We had nothing... and we got along just fine. It wasn't until Festivus 2010, after Tony Leto from the Wagner Companies read a news article[52] about my pole-less family, that he graciously arranged for a pole to be delivered to us. It was a Festivus Miracle that arrived in a long cardboard box, shipped all the way to Winnipeg from Milwaukee. We now use that pole every year. Thanks Tony!

In fact last December, on a typically cold Winnipeg winter night, I pulled that same aluminum pole out of a storage closet and dragged it to the household of my nephew Andrew and his wife Alysa. They had kindly volunteered to host our annual Festivus party. It gave them a chance to show off their new home, but more importantly, it presented an opportunity for the family to fawn over their brand new baby daughter. Prior to the gathering, the hosts had announced the theme would be "No Soup for You", so I lugged along a steaming pot of Mulligatawny soup. In fact, we all brought different soup concoctions to nosh upon: Chicken, Seafood Bisque, Turkey Chili and Cream of Broccoli to name a few. Once we were sated on soup, Andrew coerced the gathering to play a hilarious Pictionary-like game, and then we moved to the living room to open all the crap that was brought to be regifted. There were old dishes, a candleholder set, an awful looking poodle figurine (it keeps coming back every year) and a porcelain one-eyed clown doll, which I was proud to accept as my consolation prize. Afterward, there was *Seinfeld* trivia, but nobody can beat my nephews Andrew and Jason (even me). As usual, it was a hilariously one-sided trivia match.

Ten years ago, after my family had our first Festivus, I went online to find information about the holiday. I was disappointed! What I found was spread out over a variety of sites. Some of the sites were out of date, or had broken links and pages. Since I am a web designer, and I had a newfound passion for Festivus, I quickly surmised, "I can do a better job than this!" I decided to create a new web site, include all the information a person could possibly want, and then write some new humorous features as well. In November 2006, I registered the domain name FestivusWeb.com, and the site took off. Over the years, the site has grown and become more popular every year. What a load of fun!

Now, back to the pole. You may be wondering why we went so many years without a Festivus pole. It's simple. It never crossed our minds that having an aluminum pole would actually enhance the good times we were already having. We started our Festivus tradition as an impromptu party meant "for the rest of us" and we continued in that vein. Changes weren't required.

Just like the O'Keefes, our Festivus is about being together as a family. It's about being joyful and jokey. It's about eating and laughing. It's about having another reason to be together and act foolish, with no strings attached. I sincerely hope Festivus is the same for you. ~ *Mark Nelson*

Appendix A : Seinfeld Foods

You may wonder what kind of people would put so much stock in what was referred to in some *Seinfeld* episodes that ran decades ago. The answer is "fun people". If you have no sense of mirth, read no further.

This is not intended as an exhaustive list, as there were plenty of other "foods" which made an appearance in the 180 episodes of *Seinfeld*. Still, this list is one of the best references you will find if you are planning to include some Seinfeldism in your Festivus celebration.

Main Courses and Side Dishes

Bagels
After returning to work at H&H Bagels, Kramer brings day old bagels back to Jerry's. *("The Strike" – S09E10)*

Beefarino
Kramer feeds "Price Club" Beefarino to a handsom cab horse, and gives the horse indigestion. *("The Rye" – S07E11)*

Big Salad
Throughout the series, this is Elaine's favorite meal at the diner. Elaine describes it as, "a salad, only bigger, with lots of stuff in it." *("The Soup" – S06E07)*

Calzone
During a meeting, George Steinbrenner becomes intrigued when he smells George's calzone. Steinbrenner then has George bring him a calzone every day at lunch. *("The Calzone" – S07E20)*

Chinese Flounder
Elaine falls in love with a new Chinese dish, "Supreme Flounder". However, she can't place an order because she lives on the side of the street just outside the restaurant's delivery area. She soon discovers that she can place an order, but she has to receive the food in the janitor's closet in the building across the street. *("The Pothole" – S08E16)*

Cornish Game Hen
The Costanzas go to a dinner party at the Ross's (George's future in-laws) where they are served Cornish game hen. Frank makes the remark, "What is that, like a little chicken?" Later in the meal,

the perfect dinner guest Frank Costanza postulates further, "Let me understand, you got the hen, the chicken and the rooster. The rooster goes with the chicken. So, who's having sex with the hen?" *("The Rye" – S07E11)*

Crepes
Kramer loans a group of Dominican cigar rollers to the Magic Pan Crepe restaurant to roll crepes. Unfortunately, the crepes are too tightly wrapped and the hot filling squirts out, burning the patrons. Afterward, Kramer says regretfully, "Well, that's why you gotta get real Cubans." *("The English Patient" – S08E17)*

Deli Meat (Very thinly sliced)
Kramer acquires a deli slicer and begins to produce very thinly sliced meats. *("The Slicer" – S09E07)*

Egg Rolls
While waiting for a table in a Chinese restaurant, Jerry dares Elaine to steal an egg roll from a stranger's plate. *("The Chinese Restaurant" – S02E11)*

Fusilli
Kramer makes a small statue of Jerry using Fusilli pasta. *("The Fusilli Jerry" – S06E21)*

Gyro
Kramer attempts to purchase a gyro from a vendor on a subway stop, but he doesn't make it back onto the subway before the doors close. *("The Cigar Store Indian" – S05E10)*

Kung Pao Chicken
At work, George eats Kung Pao chicken. The hot food makes him sweat, and he looks guilty when Mr. Wilhelm questions him about missing equipment. George's classic response is, "It's the Kung Pao. George likes his chicken spicy." *("The Jimmy" – S06E19)*

Lobster
Kramer poaches lobsters from traps while combing the beach. *("The Hamptons" – S05E21)*

Macaroni
When Kramer visits Bette Midler in the hospital he brings a pasta statue made from macaroni. *("The Understudy" – S06E24)*

Marble Rye
After his parents quietly bring home the marble rye they had brought to a dinner party, George tries to replace the loaf of bread with the aid of Jerry and a fishing pole. *("The Rye" – S07E11)*

Mutton or Pork Chops
After ordering a salad in a restaurant, Jerry realizes that he is not coming across as very manly. Later, he lies and tells his girlfriend that he loves meat. As a result, the next two dates she serves him mutton and pork chops. Jerry's reaction is, "Hey, salad's got nuttin' on this mutton," as he hides the meat in his coat pocket. *("The Wink" – S07E04)*

Pizza (Make your own)
Kramer resurrects his make your own pizza idea and attempts to go into business with restaurateur Poppie. The result is predictably disastrous. *("The Couch" – S06E05)*

Paella
Estelle Costanza invites Jerry's parents over for a paella dinner. However, the Seinfelds do not care for the Costanzas, and they decide

not to come. Estelle laments, "What are we going to do with all this paella!" *("The Raincoats" – S05E18 and S05E19)*

Pasta Primavera
At a restaurant, Elaine sneezes on a plate of pasta primavera that is served to NBC executive Russell Dalrymple. Later, he is violently ill. *("The Shoes" – S04E16)*

Risotto
George discovers his girlfriend loves risotto more than she loves sex (with him). *("The Mango" – S05E01)*

Sausages (Home-Made)
Jerry finds Kramer and Newman in his kitchen making sausages

and playing a tape of "Mañana" by Jackie Davis. *("The Blood" – S09E04)*

Shrimp
When George overeats shrimp at a lunch meeting, one of his co-workers comments, "the ocean called, they're running out of shrimp." George spends the rest of the episode searching for a perfect comeback. *("The Comeback" – S08E13)*

T-Bone
George tries to get his co-workers to refer to him buy the nickname "T-Bone". *("The Maid" – S09E19)*

Soups

Bouillabaisse
George tells Jerry and Russel Dalrymple that the kitchen staff at "Bouchard's" were accustomed to using the bouillabaisse as a toilet. *("The Shoes" – S04E16)*

Chicken Gumbo
An example of a soup that would have constituted "being a meal". Used as an example along with Mushroom Barley and Matzah Ball. *("The Soup" – S06E07)*

Consommé
When Jerry takes Kenny Bania out for a meal, Bania orders soup and argues that soup is not a meal. Later, after it is revealed the soup he had ordered was consommé, it was agreed upon that consommé is not a meal. *("The Soup" – S06E07)*

Crab Bisque
The soup Jerry successfully orders from the Soup Nazi, and then enjoys in front of George. *("The Soup Nazi" – S07E06)*

Jambalaya
The soup Newman orders from the Soup Nazi. Afterward he runs outside, smells the bag and exclaims, "Jambalaya!" *("The Soup Nazi" – S07E06)*

Lobster Bisque
The soup Elaine refers to as the "best part" of her date. *("The Yada Yada" – S08E19)*

Matzah Ball Soup
An example of a soup that would have constituted "being a meal". Used as an example along with Mushroom Barley and Chicken

Gumbo. *("The Soup" – S06E07)*

Mulligatawny

The soup Kramer asks Elaine to buy from the Soup Nazi. Unfortunately, she fails in the quest after she does not obey the rules and is banned from buying soup. *("The Soup Nazi" – S07E06)*

Mushroom Barley

One of the soup recipes Elaine finds in the Soup Nazi's old armoire. *("The Soup Nazi" – S07E06)* Also, an example of a soup that would have constituted "being a meal". Used as an example along with Chicken Gumbo and Matzah Ball. *("The Soup" – S06E07)*

Turkey Chili

The soup George initially orders from the Soup Nazi when he is turned away for breaking the rules. *("The Soup Nazi" – S07E06)*

Wild Mushroom

One of the soup recipes Elaine finds in the Soup Nazi's old armoire. *("The Soup Nazi" – S07E06)*

Yankee Bean

The soup Elaine feeds her boyfriend Owen March, the prominent author and essayist, after he had a stroke. *("The Alternate Side" – S03E11)*

Snacks

Airline Peanuts

A famous Jerry Seinfeld comedy bit is about airline peanuts. It makes an appearance in the series when George has a flashback to Jerry saying, "What's the deal with airplane peanuts." *("The Summer of George" – S08E22)*

Bear Claws

Elaine's boyfriend found a cache of bear claw pastries while scrounging in the garbage. *("The Strongbox" – S09E14)* Newman places an order for "a pair of bear claws" at the diner. *("The Sniffing Accountant" – S05E04)*

Cheese (Large Block)

George commented that he would like to eat a block of cheese the size of a car battery. *("The Foundation" – S08E01)*

Chips Ahoy!

Morty Seinfeld's favorite cookie. When his wife admonished him for eating Chips Ahoy! he replied, "Look, I got a few good years left. If I want a Chip Ahoy, I'm having it." *("The Cadillac" – S07E14)*

Chips and Dip

At a funeral, George got caught double dipping a chip. *("The Implant" – S04E19)*

Drake's Coffee Cake

Jerry attempted to bribe Newman with a Drake's coffee cake. However, a starving Elaine devoured the cake before Newman. *("The Suicide" – S03E15)*

Muffin Tops

While eating a muffin, Elaine mentioned to her former boss, Mr. Lippman that muffin tops would be a million dollar idea. Later, she discovered Lippman had opened a muffin top store called "Top of the Muffin to You!" *("The Muffin Tops" – S08E21)*

Pizza Bagels

Kramer served pizza bagels and bite-sized Three Musketeers on his "Peterman Reality Tour". Apparently, the bagels were cinnamon raisin. *("The Muffin Tops" – S08E21)*

Poppy Seed Muffins

After Elaine's urine tested positive for opium, she soon realized the source was the poppy seeds in her favorite muffins. *("The Shower Head" – S07E16)*

Pretzels

After Kramer received a line in a Woody Allen film, saying "These pretzels are making me thirsty!", all the main characters attempted to recite the line in their own way. *("The Alternate Side" – S03E11)*

Pudding Skins Singles

George figured out how to separate the pudding skin from the pudding, and thus created "pudding skin singles". *("The Blood" – S09E04)*

Ring Dings (and Pepsi)

When discussing what to bring to a dinner party, George suggested, "I show up with Ring Dings and Pepsi, I become the biggest hit of the party." *("The Dinner Party" – S05E13)*

Soda Crackers (In a Briefcase)

When Kramer begins an office job (for no pay), he fills his briefcase with soda crackers. *("The Bizarro Jerry" – S08E03)*

Sandwiches

Atomic Sub

Elaine frequents a submarine sandwich shop enough times to complete a loyalty card that will get her a free submarine sandwich. However, she loses the card. Jerry refers to Atomic Sub as a "high-end hoagie outfit". *("The Strike" – S09E10)*

Chicken Salad on Rye

The sandwich George orders when he decides to begin doing the opposite. His complete order was, "Chicken salad, on rye, untoasted ... and a cup of tea." *("The Opposite" – S05E22)*

Pastrami Sandwich

George discovers he loves to eat during sex, and pastrami sandwiches are his favorite. Near the end of the episode, he meets Vivian who shares his views: "I find the pastrami to be the most sensual of all the salted cured meats." *("The Blood" – S09E04)*

Tuna on Toast

The sandwich George normally orders at Monk's Diner. In fact, the server knows his complete order by heart, "Tuna on toast, coleslaw, cup of coffee." *("The Opposite" – S05E22)*

Tuna Sandwich

George makes tuna sandwiches for a rock climbing date with his "boyfriend" Tony. *("The Stall" – S05E12)*

Desserts

Apple Pie

Jerry cannot understand why his girlfriend Audrey refuses to take a bite of his apple pie. She simply shakes her head "no" and does not give a reason why. *("The Pie" – S05E15)*

Black and White Cookies

When Jerry and Elaine went to Schnitzer's Bakery to purchase a chocolate babka, Jerry bought and ate a black and white cookie. As he ate the cookie he soliloquized about racial divisions, "Look to the cookie Elaine... Look to the cookie." Ironically, he vomited after eating the cookie. *("The Dinner Party" – S05E13)*

Chocolate/Cinnamon Babka

Jerry and Elaine go to Schnitzer's Bakery to purchase a chocolate babka for a dinner party. Unfortunately, the bakery is out of chocolate babka and they are forced to buy a cinnamon babka, which Elaine refers to as "lesser babka". *("The Dinner Party" – S05E13)*

Chocolate Éclairs

George had begun to impress his girlfriend's mother, until he was caught biting into a partially eaten chocolate éclair that he found in the trash. *("The Gymnast" – S06E06)*

Entenmann's

Elaine replaces Mr. Peterman's antique wedding cake with an Entenmann's cake. *("The Frogger" – S09E18)*

Huckleberry Pie

Kramer was baking a huckleberry pie at his apartment while he was heating his clothes in Jerry's oven. *("The Calzone" – S07E20)*

Ice Cream Sundae

On a televised broadcast of the US Open, George is shown eating an ice cream sundae with the dessert smeared all over his face. The announcers made fun of the scene, "Boy, I'll bet you THAT guy can cover a lot of court... Hey buddy, they got a new invention... it's called a napkin!" *("The Lip Reader" - S05E06")*

Jell-O (With cut up bananas)

Estelle Costanza makes Jell-O with cut up pieces of bananas because, "George likes the bananas!" *("The Puffy Shirt" – S05E02)*

Non-Fat Yogurt

Jerry, Elaine and George eat at a non-fat frozen yogurt shop in which Kramer has invested. Throughout the episode, they debate as to whether the yogurt is actually non-fat. *("The Non-Fat Yogurt" – S05E07)*

Pineapple Gelato

Kramer sought to purchase pineapple gelato for Bette Midler. *("The Understudy" – S06E24)*

Wedding Cake

Needing a dose of sugar, Elaine raids Mr. Peterman's refrigerator where she finds and eats a piece of cake. Later, Peterman reveals that it was an antique, from the wedding of King Edward VIII to Wallis Simpson. *("The Frogger" – S09E18)*

Fruits and Vegetables

Brocolli (Steamed)

Newman ordered steamed broccoli at the "Kenny Rogers" chicken outlet, which tipped Jerry off that Kramer was in on the order. Newman referred to the brocolli as "vile weed." *("The Chicken Roaster" – S08E08)*

Grapefruit

A piece of grapefruit pulp from Jerry's breakfast flew into George's eye and caused him to begin to wink, which caused further problems at work. Jerry denied this ever happened and claimed that pulp couldn't make it across the table, to which George replied, "Pulp can move baby!" *("The Wink" – S07E04)*

Hampton Tomatoes

On a trip to the Hamptons, George raved about the Hampton tomatoes. *("The Hamptons" – S05E21)*

Mackinaw Peaches

Kramer and Newman raved about "Mackinaw" peaches from Oregon, which were only ripe for two weeks a year. PS. They don't really exist. *("The Doodle" – S06E20)*

Mangos

George discovered that Kramer's mangoes were the cure for his sexual dysfunction. *("The Mango" – S05E01)*

Oranges

After Kramer incorrectly claims oranges are rare in Japan, George and Jerry bring a bag of oranges to a meeting with excutives from the Nakamura Broadcasting Company. *("The Checks" - S08E07)*

Plantains

When Kramer was banned from the fruit store, he directed Jerry to go to the store and buy him plantains. *("The Mango" – S05E01)*

Plums (with red on the inside)

When Kramer was banned from the fruit store, he directed Jerry to go to the store and buy him fruit. Kramer specifically ordered Jerry to get. "plums, with the red on the inside." *("The Mango" – S05E01)*

Raisins (In a box)

While taping the pilot for George and Jerry's NBC show, George was obsessed with a box of raisins that was taken by the actor who was playing Kramer. *("The Pilot" – S04E23 and S04E24)*

Beverages

Bosco

George refuses to tell anyone his secret ATM code, which was his favorite drink, "Bosco". *("The Secret Code" – S07E07)* George attempts to confront an old girlfriend who once stained his shirt with Bosco. *("The Baby Shower" – S02E10)*

Champagne Coolies

Jerry and Ethan (the Wig Master) enjoy Champagne Coolies together on an outdoor patio. *("The Wig Master" – S07E18)*

Hennigan's Scotch

Kramer drank Hennigan's just to see if the others could smell alcohol on him. The result was negative, so Kramer made a humorous endorsement, "That's right, folks. I just had three shots of Hennigan's, and I don't smell. Imagine, you can walk around drunk all day. That's Hennigan's, the no-smell, no-tell Scotch." Later in the episode, while working at his new job, George has sex with the cleaning lady after they drink Hennigan's. Too bad, Hennigan's is fictional! *("The Red Dot" – S03E12)*

Merlot

At a dinner party, it is revealed that George's mother has never heard of Merlot, as she remarked, "Merlot? I never heard of it. Did they just invent it?" *("The Rye" – S07E11)*

Ovaltine

Jerry helps fellow comedian Kenny Bania with his routine, which had included a twelve-minute bit about Ovaltine. Jerry wrote a new bit for Kenny which read, "Ovaltine, the mug is round, the jar is round, why don't they call it Roundtine." *("The Fatigues" – S08E06)*

Snapple

Jerry always had Snapple in his fridge. *("The Virgin" – S04E10)*

Yoohoo

The Bubble Boy's father drove a Yoohoo truck. *("The Bubble Boy" – S04E07)*

Condiments

Barbecue Sauce

Jerry accidentally broke a bottle of barbecue sauce that had a face that looked like Charles Grodin on the label. *("The Doll" – S07E17)*

Ketchup and Mustard in the Same Bottle

One of Kramer's ideas, which he shared with his intern Darren. *("The Voice" – S09E02)*

Maple Syrup

Jerry brings his own bottle of maple syrup to the diner. *("The Wife" – S05E17)*

Salsa

George and Jerry wasted time by discussing how salsa is now the number one condiment in America. Jerry determined the reason was because "people like to say salsa." *("The Pitch" – S04E03)*

Candy

Bite-sized Three Musketeers

Kramer served bite-sized Three Musketeers and pizza bagels on his "Peterman Reality Bus Tour". *("The Muffin Tops" – S08E21)*

Chinese Chewing Gum

Kramer insists that everyone try Lloyd Braun's Chinese chewing gum, which leads to Jerry buying one hundred dollars worth. *("The Gum" – S07E10)*

Chunky Bars

Jerry discovers Chunky Bar wrappers in his couch cushions, which leads him to believe that Newman has been in his apartment. Jerry's reaction to the discovery is, "I know the chunky that left these Chunkies! Newman!" *("The Doodle" – S06E20)*

Jujyfruits

When Elaine discovers that her boyfriend Jake Jarmel has been in an accident, she stops to buy a box of Jujyfruits before she rushes to the hospital to be by his side. *("The Opposite" – S05E22)*

Junior Mints

As they were in the operating room gallery observing the operation on Elaine's friend, Kramer offered Jerry a Junior Mint. However, Jerry refused the candy, which resulted in Kramer accidentally dropping the mint into the open incision. Kramer was upset at Jerry's refusal of the mint, "who's going to turn down a Junior Mint? It's chocolate, it's peppermint, it's delicious!" *("The Junior Mint" – S04E20)*

Oh Henry!

Elaine's old high school friend, Sue Ellen Mischke, is the heir to the O Henry! candy bar fortune. As Kramer's lawyer Jackie Chiles commented, "It's got chocolate, peanuts, nougat, it's delicious, scrumptious outstanding." *("The Caddy" – S07E12)*

Pez

At a piano recital, Jerry teased Elaine with a Tweety Bird Pez dispenser. This caused her to laugh aloud and create a disturbance. *("The Pez Dispenser" – S03E14)*

Snickers

After Elaine told the gang her boss, Mr. Pitt, eats his Snickers bar with a knife and fork, it began a disturbing new trend. *("The Pledge Drive" – S06E03)*

Tic Tacs

Elaine gives a box of Tic Tacs to her co-worker because he is a "real sidler". *("The Merv Griffin Show" – S09E06)*

Twix

George unsuccessfully attempts to buy a Twix bar from a vending machine. *("The Dealership" – S09E11)*

Fast Food

Arby's
David Puddy's favorite fast food restaurant. In fact it was the place he often took Elaine for a date, to her great chagrin. *("The Dealership" – S09E11)* Also, David Puddy loved to announce, "It feels like an Arby's night." *("The Burning" – S09E16)*

Kenny Rogers' Chicken
After a Kenny Rogers Roasters restaurant opened up across the street, both Kramer and Newman fell in love with the food. *("The Chicken Roaster" – S08E08)*

Movie Hot Dogs
Elaine expressed disgust for movie theatre hot dogs: "Movie theater hot dogs? I'd rather lick the food off the floor." *("The Chinese Restaurant" – S02E11)* Also, Kramer eats an ancient snack bar hot dog at the Alex Theatre, and then gets sick outside. *("The Gum" – S07E10)*

Papaya King
Kramer ran across the street to get a hot dog from Papaya King. *("The Movie" – S04E14)*

Breakfast

Cereal
Cereal was Jerry's favorite food, and there were various cereals on display in Jerry's apartment throughout the *Seinfeld* series. For example: Honey Comb, Cheerios, Bran Flakes, Corn Flakes, Grape Nuts, Kix, Life, Special K, Reese's Peanut Butter Puffs. *(There are more, however they are difficult to identify.)*

Corn Flakes
Jerry and his girlfriend Jeannie both enjoy cereal, including copious amounts of Corn Flakes. *("The Invitations" – S07E24)*

Egg White Omelette
At Monk's Diner, Jerry normally ordered an egg white omelet. However, when they ate at "Reggie's" the menu stated, "No egg white omelets." *("The Soup" – S06E07)*

Kasha
The *Seinfeld* gang remarked how George's parents' house smelled of Kasha. *("The Cigar Store Indian" – S05E10)* Also, when Frank moved in with George, he made his own Kasha and even offered it to George while they were in bed together. *("The Doorman" – S06E18)*

Pancakes
Jerry and his "fake" wife Meryl enjoy pancakes together. When they finally break up Jerry laments, "We'll always have pancakes." *("The Wife" – S05E17)*

Scrambled Eggs with Lobster
George got revenge on Jerry's girlfriend, Rachel, by tricking her into eating non-kosher, scrambled eggs with lobster. *("The Hamptons" – S05E21)*

Appendix B : Festivus Gift Exchange Script

This script may be used as a fun way to regift at Festivus.

Instructions

In advance, the host of the party should inform everyone to bring a wrapped gift to "regift" at the party. Make sure you tell them not to buy anything, as the whole point of the game is to "regift" something.

As the guests arrive, have the gifts placed in a common area. When it is time for the regifting, have each guest select any gift from the common area and then sit in a circle. The host should read the story and accentuate the words **LEFT**, **RIGHT** and **ACROSS** (or **CROSS**).

When left is heard, the gifts are passed to the left, when right is heard they pass to the right. When across or cross is heard, the guests exchange their gifts with a person across the circle.

The Story of Festivus

Let's begin...

It was December in New York and the *Seinfeld* gang was getting ready for the holidays. There were gifts to regift and regift again. *(The host should point at all the gifts around the room)*

However, George was surprised to receive a Festivus card from his dear old Dad. Poor George! He thought that the trauma of his childhood Festivus had been **LEFT** behind. But here it was, **RIGHT** in front of him.

George looked at the card and thought, "This is not **RIGHT**."

The card said, "Dear son, Happy Festivus."

George was **CROSS**.

Elaine asked, "What's Festivus, why so mad Georgie?"

But George didn't want to say anything about it. So Jerry explained, "Mr. Costanza hated all the commercial and religious aspects of Christmas, so he made up his own holiday. Instead of a tree his father put up an aluminum pole. And weren't there feats of strength that always **LEFT** you crying?"

George was upset "I can't take it anymore! Are you happy now?!" Then he gathered his things and **LEFT** the coffee shop.

Later, Kramer heard about Festivus and he was intrigued. After all he was down **RIGHT** interested in all things zany and inane. Kramer contacted Frank Costanza to inquire about Festivus. Frank was happy to oblige Kramer and gave an explanation of how Festivus was invented.

"Many Christmases ago, I went to buy a doll for my son. I reached for the last one they had - but so did another man. As I rained blows upon him, I realized there had to be another way!"

Kramer blurted out, "that must have been some kind of doll". He was **RIGHT.** She was!

Frank continued his story "The doll was destroyed. But out of that, a new holiday was born. A Festivus for the rest of us!"

Now Frank was inspired. Before he **LEFT**, he informed Kramer that he was planning to resurrect Festivus.

He scurried off to fetch the Festivus pole from where he had **LEFT** it... **RIGHT** in the crawlspace.

Frank dragged the pole **ACROSS** town to the coffee shop to announce to his son George that Festivus was reborn.

When George saw the pole he was upset. George was even more upset when Frank produced a tape player from his **RIGHT** coat pocket.

Frank pressed play and an insane scene from a past Festivus was heard. George ran out of the cafe sobbing. Frank sighed, "We had some good times."

That very night, Festivus was held. George brought his boss, Mr. Kruger along, just to prove to him how screwed up his family really was.

Jerry arrived without his girlfriend, Gwen, the "Two-Face". Why was she called Two-Face? That's a story better **LEFT** for another time.

Elaine was also there, and she was so surprised to see that Kramer had brought along her two bookie friends from the OTB **ACROSS** town. Kramer declared the surprise to be a Festivus Miracle; however no miracle would help her horse, Captain Nemo, who had lost the race and apparently had been shot.

Mr. Kruger was also interested in learning more about the Festivus pole. Frank explained, "It's made from aluminum. Very high strength-to-weight ratio." This **LEFT** Mr. Kruger dumbfounded. He exclaimed that Frank's "Belief system was fascinating".

Finally, dinner was served and Frank addressed the gathering, "Welcome, newcomers. The tradition of Festivus begins with the airing of grievances. I've got a lot of problems with you people! And now you're gonna hear about it! You, Kruger! My son tells me your company stinks!"

George moaned, "Oh, God."

Frank continued, "Quiet George, you'll get yours in a minute. Kruger, you couldn't smooth a silk sheet if you had a hot date with a babe..." Then Frank looked confused and sputtered, "I lost my train of thought."

Everyone looked **ACROSS** the dining room table at each other and wondered where Frank may have **LEFT** it. Still, they were **LEFT** thankful that no additional grievances were aired.

Finally it was time for the Feats of Strength. Frank indicated that it was Kramer's turn to participate, but Kramer had to go, so he **LEFT**.

Everybody wondered, "Who's going to do the Feats of Strength?"

Just then, Mr. Kruger recommended, "How about George?"

"Good thinking Kruger", Frank replied. Then he removed his sweater and looked **ACROSS** the table at George.

Frank yelled out the challenge "Let's Rumble!"

"You can take him Georgie", Estelle Costanza was heard to encourage her son.

As we fade away from Festivus at the Costanza household we are **LEFT** with the memory of George moaning "Oh, come on! Be sensible!", and Frank goading him with "Stop crying, and fight your father!"

The end!

Now look at the gift you have in front of you. Does anyone have the same gift they brought? If it is the same gift you brought, then swap it with the person on your LEFT.

Open the gifts one at a time. Make sure you show everybody what kind of crap you received.

Appendix C : Festivus Glossary

18 December 1997
The original air date of the *Seinfeld* episode "The Strike", the episode which featured Festivus as a sub-plot. This is the birthdate of modern day Festivus.

23 December
The date in which Frank Costanza tells Kramer that Festivus was to occur. As a result, this has become the official date of Festivus.

Airing of Grievances
The time at Festivus where you have the opportunity to tell everyone how he or she has disappointed you in the past year.

A Festivus for the Rest of Us!
The traditional slogan for Festivus. Its meaning can be varied and it can be applied to many different situations. However, when Frank Costanza uttered the phrase he meant that Festivus is a secular holiday, with no religious or social boundaries.

Aluminum
The metal that comprises Festivus poles. Known for its high strength-to-weight ratio.

Atomic Sub
The name of the submarine sandwich shop Elaine prefers to frequent. Jerry refers to it as a "High End Hoagie Outfit."

Bagel Technician
The description of Kramer's position on his bagel shop business cards.

Bayside
George made a claim that his family had been kicked out of Bayside for their Festivus beliefs. Bayside is a real place, an upper middle class neighbourhood in Queens, Long Island. Meanwhile, George's story is complete tripe.

Beer Can Festivus Pole
One method some have used is to stack empty beer cans together to form a Festivus "pole". Some have derided it for its lack of authenticity, while others have marveled at its ingenuity and cheapness. Still, others

drank the beer and then forgot what they were doing.

Belief System

How Mr. Kruger interprets Frank's choice of an aluminum pole as the chief symbol of Festivus. Kruger describes it to be "fascinating".

Blimey

The exclamation of surprise Elaine uses when she realized "Denim Vest" gave her a fake phone number. The word is derived from the olde English saying, "God Blind Me"... which leads us to believe Elaine must have lived in a London orphanage as a child.

Blow off Number

A fake phone number Elaine uses to thwart unwanted suitors.

Captain Nemo

The name of the horse upon which Elaine places a bet. We heard he is not feeling well. We just hope he is doing okay.

Cassette Tapes

In both the Costanza and O'Keefe families, the father keeps audio cassette recordings of past Festivus celebrations as a record of the proceedings.

Children's Alliance

The charity in which Tim Whatley donated to in the name of his friends, as a Hanukkah gift. In comparison to The Human Fund (George's fake charity), the Children's Alliance was a real charity,

Clock

The original O'Keefe family Festivus featured a clock and a bag. Sometimes the clock was placed in the bag and hung on the wall. Why? That's not for you to know!

Cloning Sheep

The reference Jerry uses to indicate that it is currently modern times. e.g. "They're cloning sheep now."

Costanza

In the fictional world of *Seinfeld*, the surname of the family who had a penchant for celebrating Festivus.

Cougar

At his family's Festivus dinner, this is how Frank Costanza often referred to Mr. Kruger.

Crawlspace

Typically, a place to store your aluminum pole once Festivus is complete. In fact, this is where Frank Costanza tells people he stores his pole. If it's good enough for the Costanzas it should be good enough for everyone else.

Dan O'Keefe
The writer responsible for including his family's Festivus traditions in the *Seinfeld* episode "The Strike". Son of Daniel O'Keefe Sr..

Daniel O'Keefe Sr.
The father of the O'Keefe clan, and the man credited for unilaterally inventing the Festivus holiday sometime in 1966.

Daniel von Bargen
The actor who played Mr. Kruger in the Festivus episode "The Strike". He was featured in other *Seinfeld* episodes as the same character, and is highly recognizable as an actor, as he had roles in many other television shows and major motion pictures. Sadly, he passed away on March 1, 2015.

Denim Vest
The nickname Elaine gives to a potential suitor who is wearing a "Denim Vest" (Played by Kevin McDonald). Incidentally, those aren't buttons. They're snaps.

Distracted
The general feeling Frank Costanza has when he sees tinsel.

Doctor van Nostrand
Kramer's alter ego, recognized as such by Mr. Kruger from their previous meeting in "The Slicer" (*S09E07*). See page 36.

Doll Shopping (for a Son)
The very activity in which Frank Costanza was partaking when he came to realize there had to be a better way. That must have been some kind of doll! (She was...)

Fake Phone Number
The method of avoidance Elaine employed to dissuade romantic suitors whom she considered to be less spongeworthy.

Feats of Strength
Festivus always ends with the Feats of Strength. Festivus is not over until the head of the household is pinned.

Feminist
How George's boss, Mr. Kruger, interprets the word "Festivus" the first time he hears it.

Festivus
Made popular by the *Seinfeld* episode "The Strike", Festivus is a secular holiday that was initially celebrated by the O'Keefe family, mainly in the 1970s and 1980s.

Festivus Dinner
An important part of the Festivus tradition, the Festivus Dinner is

where you gather your family and friends and tell them all the ways they've disappointed you in the past year.

Festivus is Your Heritage
This was how Frank Costanza explained to his son that he should not disparage Festivus. Normally followed by the phrase, "It's part of who you are."

Festivus Miracle
The classification of any innocuous occurrence during Festivus, which one might wish to elevate to a special status.

Festivus Restivus
A shortened version of the phrase, "a Festivus for the rest of us." It is an increasingly popular Festivus related slogan.

Festivus yes! Bagels no!
The slogan on Kramer's picket sign when he goes on strike from the bagel shop demanding a day off to celebrate Festivus.

Festivusite
One who celebrates Festivus.

Flask
A flask is the item that Mr. Kruger pulls from his suit jacket and opens as the Festivus dinner is underway. In fact, it is the only appearance of alcohol in the Costanza Festivus celebration.

Fright Night
How Kramer described Elaine when he saw her outside the bagel shop, when her mascara had run and her hair was all moist and squiddy. e.g. "It's fright night!"

Gwen
The first name of Jerry's girlfriend in the Festivus episode. She is a beautiful woman, however her looks seem to diminish in poor lighting. For this reason, George nicknames her "Two-Face".

H&H Bagels
The bagel shop where it was discovered that Kramer once worked, prior to going on strike for higher wages.

Happy Festivus
The traditional Festivus greeting, deemed so because the greeting is specifically used in the *Seinfeld* episode. e.g. Elaine: "Happy Festivus Georgie!"

Head of the Household
An important figure in Festivus tradition, as it is implied Festivus does not end until the "Head of the Household" is pinned.

Human Fund
A fictitious charity invented by George Costanza in an effort to appear that he

is giving out generous Christmas gifts where he is actually only giving away a fake greeting card with the corny slogan "Money for People".

It has a Certain Understated Stupidity

This is how Jerry describes George's plan to give out fake "Human Fund" cards to his co-workers. George then attributed the line to the Clint Eastwood movie *The Outlaw Josey Wales.* Smart movie buffs will tell you that George was wrong, and the line isn't in the movie. This turns out to be the actual joke.

Kick Ass Philanthropist

George claimed that he would not only be a good philanthropist, he would be a kick ass philanthropist.

Kruger

Played by actor Daniel von Bargen, Mr. Kruger is the CEO of "Kruger Industrial Smoothing" and George Costanza's boss. When he accuses George of inventing the "Human Fund" charity, George uses Festivus as a vague excuse. As a result, Kruger forces George to prove that Festivus exists.

Kruger Industrial Smoothing

The wildly ineffective company in which George Costanza works. According to George, their motto is, "We don't care, and it shows."

Let's Rumble!

The exclamation Frank utters just prior to beginning the Feats of Strength.

Meatloaf

The meal Estelle Costanza served at her family Festivus dinner. It seems to be better when served on a bed of lettuce.

Money for People

The slogan for the "Human Fund", the made-up charity invented by George Costanza.

Newcomers

How Frank Costanza refers to guests who attend his family's Festivus celebration.

No Bagel!

The verbal slogan Kramer uses when he is on strike from H&H Bagels.

No Elaine

For potential suitors she finds unspongeworthy, Elaine used a blow off number that spelled out "N-O E-L-A-I-N-E". This made eight digits, however Elaine also explained how the extra "e" is for "ech".

No, Not the Feats of Strength

George Costanza's lament, uttered when his father announced it was time for the "Festivus Feats of Strength".

O'Keefe

The surname of the family who had a penchant for celebrating Festivus in the real world of 1970s/1980s Chappaqua, New York. The family consists of parents Daniel and Deborah, plus three sons: Dan, Larry and Mark.

OTB

Short for Off-Track Betting. It is the location with the same phone number Elaine has been giving out to rid herself of undesirable suitors.

PBR

Acronym meaning "Pabst Blue Ribbon", the favorite beer of Daniel O'Keefe Sr., and a popular beer for producing beer can Festivus poles.

Pepperidge Farm

The brand name of the cake that was often served during the O'Keefe family's Festivus celebrations. Mrs. O'Keefe would also decorate the cake with M&Ms.

Pinned

Festivus doesn't end until the head of the household is pinned, as implied by the words of Frank Costanza in the *Seinfeld* episode "The Strike".

Porch

An entrance to a house in Queens. Notorious for its bad lighting.

Professor Highbrow

This is how Kramer refers to Jerry when he enquires why Kramer is reading a VCR manual. e.g. "Well, we can't all be reading the classics, Professor Highbrow."

Prolific

How Kramer described Frank Costanza when he learned how Frank invented Festivus.

Pulling a Whatley

How George Costanza refers to the perceived cheapskate activity of fellow *Seinfeld* character Tim Whatley. Apparently, George gave Tim Whatley Yankees tickets, and Whatley returned the favor by giving George a card that stated he had made a donation to a charity in George's name.

Rained Blows

Frank Costanza's preferred method of accosting another man when fighting over a doll.

Sawbuck

The amount you offer to bet on a horse when trying to pretend you are hip at an NYC Off-Track Betting location.

Schvitz

This is how Elaine described the steam-filled bagel shop which actively contributed to the ruination of her hair and makeup. Aside from referring to a sauna or steam bath, Schvitz is actually a Yiddish term which means "to sweat".

Seinfeldism

A catchphrase that's been used on the TV show *Seinfeld* or a demonstration of an inordinate love for the television series *Seinfeld*.

Seinfeldist

One who practices Seinfeldism.

Silk Sheet

A good example of a random item which might require smoothing, if a smoothing company was actually good at smoothing something.

Spaghetti

A dish that may be served at a traditional Festivus Dinner. At one time, many *Seinfeld* fans identified the dish served by Estelle Costanza at the Costanza Festivus as spaghetti. However, with the advent of high-definition television it was more clearly identified as meatloaf.

Stop Crying and Fight Your Father

Frank Costanza uses this taunt in an attempt to encourage his son to perform the Feats of Strength.

Strength-to-Weight Ratio

An important variable that is used to measure the worthiness of any metal. According to Frank Costanza, aluminum has a high strength-to-weight ratio.

Strike (The)

The episode of *Seinfeld* which featured Festivus as a sub-plot. It is episode 10 of Season 9, the final season of *Seinfeld*.

Studio 54 with a Menorah

This is how Elaine describes Tim Whatley's Hanukkah party at the very beginning of the *Seinfeld* episode "The Strike".

Submarine Captain

The promised rank allocated to anyone who eats ten subs at Atomic Submarine. The rank allows the person to eat a free sub, and then be immediately demoted back to regular person status. Elaine almost became a Submarine Captain, but she lost her card. Blimey.

Tape Recorder

In the original Festivus practiced by the O'Keefe family, the proceedings were recorded on a cassette tape. In the *Seinfeld* episode this element is recreated, with Frank Costanza playing the tapes of Festivus past (which left George sobbing).

Tinsel

A shiny decoration which Frank Costanza finds distracting, despite the fact he has it hanging on the walls inside his house. It's no wonder he loses his train of thought so much.

Tomcat

How Kramer referred to Jerry when he incorrectly revealed to Gwen that Jerry had another girlfriend. e.g. "Oh, he's a tomcat."

Train of Thought

An important state of mind to retain when attempting to air an extremely convoluted grievance. If you lose your train of thought, you're liable to look like a crazy old man.

Two-Face

The quaint nickname that George invents for Jerry's girlfriend Gwen, a woman who is normally attractive, but appears much less appealing in bad light, such as on the porch.

Two Bookies

When Elaine visits the off-track betting location, she meets two bookies who tell her she is notorious for all the men who have been calling and trying to get in contact with her.

Unadorned

A word commonly used to describe the state of a traditional Festivus pole.

Wagner Pole

A Festivus pole manufactured and sold by The Wagner Companies of Milwaukee, Wisconsin.

We Don't Care and it Shows

According to George, this is the motto of Kruger Industrial Smoothing.

Yamahama

What Kramer exclaimed once he saw Elaine after she had spent time in the steam-filled bagel shop, which had caused her hair to be wet and flattened, and her mascara to run.

You're Weak

On the tapes of Festivus past, this was the response given to George when he complained that he needed his glasses.

Appendix D: Festivus Quiz

Answers are on the next page. No peeking!

1. **What is the official date of Festivus?**

    a. July 4th
    b. There is no official date
    c. December 25th
    d. December 23rd

2. **Why did Frank Costanza choose an unadorned aluminum pole as his Festivus icon?**

    a. He found tinsel distracting
    b. He marvelled at the strength to weight ratio of aluminum
    c. A pole requires no decorations
    d. All of the above

3. **Who was Elaine's date at the Costanza Festivus dinner?**

    a. Jerry
    b. Denim Vest Guy
    c. Two Bookies
    d. Puddy

4. **What was the quaint nickname for Jerry's girlfriend in the *Seinfeld* Festivus episode?**

    a. Two-Face
    b. Mulva
    c. Close Talker
    d. Low Talker

5. **How many Festivus Miracles did Kramer manifest during the *Seinfeld* Festivus episode?**

    a. 1
    b. 2
    c. 3
    d. 4

6. **What was the name of the fake charity invented by George?**

   a. The Human Miracle Fund
   b. The Human Race
   c. A Human Charity
   d. The Human Fund

7. **According to Frank Costanza, what is the purpose of the Airing of Grievances?**

   a. You tell people all the ways they have disappointed you over the past year
   b. You complain about the government
   c. You argue about traffic tickets
   d. You fight with your wife

8. **According to Frank Costanza, Festivus was born when many Christmases ago he went to buy something for his son. What was he intending to buy?**

   a. Glasses
   b. A doll
   c. A Parcheesi game
   d. Kasha

9. **When is Festivus over?**

   a. Once the beverages are finished
   b. Once the airing of grievances is complete
   c. Once all the men take their pants off and play pool
   d. Once the head of the household is pinned

10. **Who did George bring to the Festivus dinner and why?**

    a. He brought his boss Mr. Kruger, to show him that Festivus was real
    b. He brought Newman, in exchange for Chunky Bars
    c. He brought his boss Mr. Kruger, to show his parents how bad Kruger and his company were
    d. He brought Uncle Leo, because Leo had Jerry's watch

Answers: 1(d), 2(d), 3(c), 4(a), 5(b), 6(d), 7(a), 8(b), 9(d), 10(a)

Endnotes

1. "Inside Look - The Strike", *Seinfeld: Season 9* [DVD], United States, Sony Pictures Home Entertainment.

2. Dan O'Keefe, "Festivus 2009: Holiday creator Dan O'Keefe takes your questions," *The Washington Post*, Dec. 21, 2009, (http://www.washingtonpost.com/wp-dyn/content/discussion/2009/12/16/DI2009121603245.html).

3. Dan O'Keefe, "Festivus 2009: Holiday creator Dan O'Keefe takes your questions," *The Washington Post*, Dec. 21, 2009, (http://www.washingtonpost.com/wp-dyn/content/discussion/2009/12/16/DI2009121603245.html).

4. "Inside Look - The Strike", *Seinfeld: Season 9* [DVD], United States, Sony Pictures Home Entertainment.

5. Dan O'Keefe, "New Day", *CNN*, Dec. 24, 2013.

6. Allen Salkin, "Fooey to the World: Festivus Is Come," *New York Times*, Dec. 19, 2004 (http://www.nytimes.com/2004/12/19/fashion/19FEST.html).

7. "Inside Look - The Strike", *Seinfeld: Season 9* [DVD], United States, Sony Pictures Home Entertainment.

8. Asawin Suebsaeng, "'Seinfeld' Writer Takes on Conservative Outrage Over Holiday Festivus Pole Protests," *Mother Jones,* Dec. 12, 2013, (http://www.motherjones.com/mojo/2013/12/festivus-pole-protest-christmas-seinfeld-dan-okeefe-fox-news).

9. "Inside Look - The Strike", *Seinfeld: Season 9* [DVD], United States, Sony Pictures Home Entertainment.

10. "Inside Look - The Strike", *Seinfeld: Season 9* [DVD], United States, Sony Pictures Home Entertainment.

11. "Notes About Nothing", *Seinfeld: Season 9* [DVD], United States, Sony Pictures Home Entertainment.

12. "Inside Look - The Strike", *Seinfeld: Season 9* [DVD], United States, Sony Pictures Home Entertainment.

13. "Notes About Nothing", *Seinfeld: Season 9* [DVD], United States, Sony Pictures Home Entertainment.

14. "Inside Look - The Strike", *Seinfeld: Season 9* [DVD], United States, Sony Pictures Home Entertainment.

15. "Inside Look - The Strike", *Seinfeld: Season 9* [DVD], United States, Sony Pictures Home Entertainment.

16. "Notes About Nothing", *Seinfeld: Season 9* [DVD], United States, Sony Pictures Home Entertainment.

17. "Notes About Nothing", *Seinfeld: Season 9* [DVD], United States, Sony Pictures Home Entertainment.

18. "Notes About Nothing", *Seinfeld: Season 9* [DVD], United States, Sony Pictures Home Entertainment.

19. "Notes About Nothing", *Seinfeld: Season 9* [DVD], United States, Sony Pictures Home Entertainment.

20. "Notes About Nothing", *Seinfeld: Season 9* [DVD], United States, Sony Pictures Home Entertainment.

21. "Notes About Nothing", *Seinfeld: Season 9* [DVD], United States, Sony Pictures Home Entertainment.

22. "Not That There's Anything Wrong With That (Outtakes and Bloopers)", *Seinfeld: Season 9* [DVD], United States, Sony Pictures Home Entertainment.

23. "Notes About Nothing", *Seinfeld: Season 9* [DVD], United States, Sony Pictures Home Entertainment.

24. "Notes About Nothing", *Seinfeld: Season 9* [DVD], United States, Sony Pictures Home Entertainment.

25. "Notes About Nothing", *Seinfeld: Season 9* [DVD], United States, Sony Pictures Home Entertainment.

26. "Notes About Nothing", *Seinfeld: Season 9* [DVD], United States, Sony Pictures Home Entertainment.

27. "Inside Look - The Strike", *Seinfeld: Season 9* [DVD], United States, Sony Pictures Home Entertainment.

28. "Notes About Nothing", *Seinfeld: Season 9* [DVD], United States, Sony Pictures Home Entertainment.

29. Asawin Suebsaeng, "'Seinfeld' Writer Takes on Conservative Outrage Over Holiday Festivus Pole Protests," *Mother Jones,* Dec. 12, 2013, (http://www.motherjones.com/mojo/2013/12/festivus-pole-protest-christmas-seinfeld-dan-okeefe-fox-news).

30. "Notes About Nothing", *Seinfeld: Season 9* [DVD], United States, Sony Pictures Home Entertainment.

31. "Inside Look - The Strike", *Seinfeld: Season 9* [DVD], United States, Sony Pictures Home Entertainment.

32. David Edwards, "'Seinfeld' Festivus writer airs grievances: Rand Paul is Bob Hope dressing up as the Fonz," *Raw Story*, Dec. 24, 2013, (http://www.rawstory.com/rs/2013/12/seinfeld-festivus-writer-airs-grievances-rand-paul-is-bob-hope-dressing-up-as-the-fonz/).

33. Sarah LeTrent, "Happy Festivus! Now air your grievances," *CNN.com*, Dec. 23, 2014 (http://www.cnn.com/2014/12/23/living/festivus-december-23-origins/).

34. Oscar Villalon, "1, 2, 3, 4, I declare a thumb war," *San Francisco Chronicle*, Dec. 8, 2003, (http://www.sfgate.com/entertainment/article/1-2-3-4-I-declare-a-thumb-war-2509691.php).

35. "Inside Look - The Strike", *Seinfeld: Season 9* [DVD], United States, Sony Pictures Home Entertainment.

36. "Inside Look - The Strike", *Seinfeld: Season 9* [DVD], United States, Sony Pictures Home Entertainment.

37. Stephen Kurczy, "Festivus becomes worldwide holiday. Break out the Festivus pole!", *Christian Science Monitor*, Dec 23, 2010, (http://www.csmonitor.com/World/Global-News/2010/1223/Festivus-becomes-worldwide-holiday.-Break-out-the-Festivus-pole!-video).

38. "Inside Look - The Strike", *Seinfeld: Season 9* [DVD], United States, Sony Pictures Home Entertainment.

39. Amanda Kooser, "Google generates Festivus pole search results for the rest of us," *CNET Magazine,* Dec. 12, 2012, (http://www.cnet.com/news/google-generates-festivus-pole-search-results-for-the-rest-of-us/)

40. Dan O'Keefe, "Festivus 2009: Holiday creator Dan O'Keefe takes your questions," *The Washington Post*, Dec. 21, 2009, (http://www.washingtonpost.com/wp-dyn/content/discussion/2009/12/16/DI2009121603245.html).

41. "Have We Lost Sight of the True Meaning of Festivus?" *Vocativ.com*, Dec. 23, 2013, (http://www.vocativ.com/culture/religion/war-festivus/).

42. Dan Perlman, "Our Visit to New York's Seinfeld: The Apartment Experience", *The Interrobang*, 2 July 2015, (http://theinterrobang.com/our-visit-to-new-yorks-seinfeld-the-apartment-experience/)

43. Maraithe Thomas, "My afternoon at the Seinfeld apartment", *The Guardian*, 26 June 2015, (http://www.theguardian.com/tv-and-radio/2015/jun/26/seinfeld-apartment-apartment-replica-new-york)

44. Julia Rose, "'Festivus' Celebration Held at Utica Fire Station," *CNYhomepage.com*, Dec. 23, 2014, (http://www.cnyhomepage.com/story/d/story/festivus-celebration-held-at-utica-fire-station/24751/6l2y_jUo50e0-0V4Jb2J9A).

45. "Public prayers: a mayor's response," *CBC Radio*, May 3, 2015, (http://www.cbc.ca/radio/the180/animal-testing-gender-wage-gap-ecomodernist-manifesto-1.3052639/public-prayers-a-mayor-s-response-1.3052891).

46. Gretchen Carlson, *The Real Story with Gretchen Carlson*, Fox News Channel, Tuesday 10 December 2013.

47. Asawin Suebsaeng, "'Seinfeld' Writer Takes on Conservative Outrage Over Holiday Festivus Pole Protests," *Mother Jones,* Dec. 12, 2013, (http://www.motherjones.com/mojo/2013/12/festivus-pole-protest-christmas-seinfeld-dan-okeefe-fox-news).

48. Stephen Colbert, *The Colbert Report*, Wednesday, 11 Dec 2013.

49. Mike Dorf, "The War on Festivus", *Dorf on Law*, Dec. 18, 2013, (http://www.dorfonlaw.org/2013/12/the-war-on-festivus.html).

50. "Have We Lost Sight of the True Meaning of Festivus?" *Vocativ.com*, Dec. 23, 2013, (http://www.vocativ.com/culture/religion/war-festivus/).

51. "Have We Lost Sight of the True Meaning of Festivus?" *Vocativ.com*, Dec. 23, 2013, (http://www.vocativ.com/culture/religion/war-festivus/).

52. Mary Ann Albright, "Festivus ... for the rest of us - 'Holiday' popularized by 'Seinfeld' enjoys lighthearted following", *The Columbian*, Dec. 20, 2010, (http://www.columbian.com/news/2010/dec/20/festivus-for-the-rest-of-us-holiday-popularized-by/).

Photo Credits

Cover: The festivus pole, unadorned and non-lit, by Matthew Keefe. 13 January 2009. Wikimedia commons image https://commons.wikimedia.org/wiki/File:Festivus_Pole.jpg Used under Creative Commons License.

P10: Festivus pole in front yard of John M. Bunch, Tampa Florida. Photo by John "Jack" M. Bunch, III. Used with permission.

P23: A clock and a bag. Photo by Mark Nelson.

P24: A clock in a bag on the wall. Photo by Mark Nelson.

P26: Tape recorder. Photo by Mark Nelson.

P27: Dunce cap in the Victorian schoolroom at the Museum of Lincolnshire Life, Lincoln, England. Wikimedia commons image http://commons.wikimedia.org/wiki/File:Museum_of_Lincolnshire_Life,_Lincoln,_England_-_DSCF1726.JPG. Used under Creative Commons License.

P28: Happy Festivus cake. Photo by Mark Nelson.

P42: Festivus Pole. Photo by Mark Nelson.

P45: Festivus poles at Home Depot. Photo by Mark Nelson

P47: Festivus poles being packaged. Photo courtesy of R & B Wagner, Inc. Used with permission.

P49: Festivus pole word cloud. Generated using wordle.com

P52: "Stripperpole" by ThemavenStripper. Wikimedia commons image. http://commons.wikimedia.org/wiki/File:Stripperpole.jpg . Used under Creative Commons License.

P53: Beer can Festivus pole. Taken on December 24, 2007 by Keith. https://www.flickr.com/photos/outofideas/2134329002. Used under Creative Commons License.

P54: Festivus Pole in New Orleans. Wikimedia commons image. http://commons.wikimedia.org/wiki/File:Festivus_Pole_in_New_Orleans.jpg. Used under Creative Commons License.

P55: Festivus pole by Danny & Chrissy. Uploaded by Flickr user weaselfactory. https://www.flickr.com/photos/magnusandfriends/6412186743/. Used with permission.

P56: Meatloaf served Estelle Costanza style. Photo by Mark Nelson.

P59: Marble rye bread, sliced and ready. Photo by Mark Nelson.

P61: Bowl of Mulligatawny accompanied by *Seinfeld* items. Photo by Mark Nelson.

P63: Vegan Black and White Cookies. Creative Commons Image by Mattie Hagedorn https://www.flickr.com/photos/vegan-baking/8746950188/. Used under Creative Commons License.

P69: Miniature Pole. Photo by Mark Nelson.

P73: "Sad orangutan & stripper pole", Berlin Zoo, 03/31/07. Uploaded by Flickr User nayrb7. https://www.flickr.com/photos/nayrb7/450008049/. Used under Creative Commons License.

P77: "Pankratiasten im Bodenkampf" by MatthiasKabel . Wikimedia commons image. http://commons.wikimedia.org/wiki/File:Pankratiasten_in_fight_copy_of_greek_statue_3_century_bC.jpg. Used under Creative Commons License.

P79: "Andrew begins the Feats of Strength" by Ian Muir. Wikimedia commons image downloaded 7 Jan 15. http://commons.wikimedia.org/wiki/File:Festivus_-_Andrew_begins_the_feats_of_strength.jpg. Used under Creative Commons License.

P80: "Festivus feats of strength" by kellypuffs. Wikimedia Commons photo downloaded 7 Jan 15. Author Kelly Puffs. http://commons.wikimedia.org/wiki/File:Festivus_feats_of_strength.jpg Used under Creative Commons License.

P80: "Me and Allison thumb wrestling" by Jeff. Wikimedia Commons: http://commons.wikimedia.org/wiki/File:Thumb_Wrestling.jpg. Used under Creative Commons License.

P82: "Blowing bubbles to mark Feats of Strength". Photo by Adam. Wikimedia Commons: http://commons.wikimedia.org/wiki/File:Festivus_Feats_of_Strength.jpg. Used under Creative Commons License.

P84: "Wrestling with a trained bear" by Library and Archives Canada. Wikimedia Commons: http://commons.wikimedia.org/wiki/File:Person_wrestling_with_a_trained_bear.jpg. Used under Creative Commons License.

P85: Louis Cyr - the famous strength athlete from Canada. Wikimedia commons image. http://upload.wikimedia.org/wikipedia/commons/d/d5/Louis_Cyr.JPG Used under Creative Commons License.

P87: Festivus Miracle graphic by Mark Nelson.

P89: Human fund card by Mark Nelson.

P92: Ugly poodle statuette, taken at my sister's place. Photo by Mark Nelson.

P94: Fat wallet photo. Photo by Mark Nelson. Wallet property of Mark "Lopsided" Nelson.

P95: Preztel bowl photo by Kimberly Vardeman. Taken on December 19, 2010. https://www.flickr.com/photos/kimberlykv/5283321290. Used under Creative Commons License.

P108: Stripper street pole by Elislike. Wikimedia commons image. http://commons.wikimedia.org/wiki/File:Streetpoleplaca.jpg Used under Creative Commons License.

P111: Festivus in Adams Morgan. Photo by Mike McKay. Wikimedia commons image. http://commons.wikimedia.org/wiki/File:Festivus_in_Adams_Morgan.jpg Used under Creative Commons License.

P116: Frank Costanza action figure image courtesy of Vinyl Sugar.

P120: Amelia and Gloria Tuckwiller. Photo by Amelia Tuckwiller. Used with permission.

P122: Photos from Kandahar by Aulton White. Used with permission.

P123: Heather S. and her family. Photo by Heather S. Used with permission.

P124: Festivus 5K logo provided by Festivus 5K for Autism. Used with permission.

P125: Soup Nazi photo by John Andrews of Creative Salem. Provided by Cindy Johnson and used with permission.

P126: Women's 5K Winner photo by Cindy Johnson. Used with permission.

P128: Lara and Steve's pole photo provided by Lara and Steve. Used with permission.

P130: Meaghan's Invition provided by Meaghan Tuohey. Used with permission.

P132: "Welcome to the party about NOTHING" photo provided by Michelle L., and used with permission.

P132: Hannah photo provided by Michelle L., and used with permission.

P133: Moops Trivia photo provided by Michelle L., and used with permission.

P133: Bathroom sign photo provided by Michelle L., and used with permission.

P133: PEZ party favor bowl photo provided by Michelle L., and used with permission.

P135: Dillsburg Festivus pole provided by Paul Tucker. Used with permission.

P137: Festivus Path photo provided by the Sydney Atheists. Uploaded by Chau. Used with Permission.

P138: Sydney Clock Throwers photo provided by the Sydney Atheists. Uploaded by Chau. Used with Permission.

P138: Sydney Grievances photo provided by the Sydney Atheists. Uploaded by Chau. Used with Permission.

P139: Little Jerry's exterior photo provided by Tara Valadez. Used with Permission.

P140: Both grievances on the pole photos provided by Tara Valadez. Used with Permission.

P140: Little Jerry's *Seinfeld* Scrabble board photo provided by Tara Valadez. Used with Permission.

P141: Grey Lodge Pub exterior photo by Mike Scotese, used with permission.

P142: Big Mug O'Pennies photo by Mike Scotese, used with permission.

P144: Spaghetti monster with pole. Graphic by Bianca. Used with permission.

P145: Sack of nickels photo. Photo by Bianca. Used with permission.

P148: NYC - Morningside Heights: Tom's Restaurant, by Wally Gobetz. Wikimedia commons image http://commons.wikimedia.org/wiki/File:Tom%27s_Restaurant,_Seinfeld.jpg. Used under Creative Commons License.

P151: Keith Hernandez "Magic Loogie" Bobblehead photo provided by Twitter user @ KerithBurke - Kerith Burke. Used with Permission.

P153: Bakersfield Condors Puffy Jersey graphic courtesy of Bakersfield Condor's press release September 3, 2014 (http://www.bakersfieldcondors.com/news/seinfeld-puffy-shirt-jerseys-on-nov-16/)

P155: Jerry's Apartment photo by Downtowngal. 26 February 2013. Wikimedia Commons image https://commons.wikimedia.org/wiki/File:757_New_Hampshire_Ave_2.jpg. Used under Creative Commons License.

P156: The Puffy Shirt from Seinfeld displayed at the National Museum of American History, by Narith5. Wikimedia Commons image https://commons.wikimedia.org/wiki/File:Smithsonian_National_Museum_of_American_History_-_Seinfeld_The_Puffy_Shirt_(120435360).jpg. Used under Creative Commons License.

P166: One-Eyed Clown statuette photo by Mark Nelson.

Word cloud images were generated through wordle.com.

Kudos to all those who make digital photography available for re-use through Creative Commons licensing. Original images created for this book are also available to be used by others under Creative Commons license: flickr.com/photos/88531684@N03/ (flickr.com user "festivusweb")

Acknowledgements

I would like to thank those who have helped make this book come to life. In no special order: Tony Leto, Joel Kopischke, Amelia Tuckwiller, Aulton White, Heather S., Cindy Johnson, Lara and Steve, Meaghan Tuohey, Michelle L., Paul Tucker, Tara Valadez, Anthony Valadez, Steve Marton, Morgan Storey, Mike "Scoats" Scotese, Diane McLean, Bianca H., Chrissy and Danny, Kerith Burke, John M. Bunch, Mike Burns. Thanks!

A special thank you to *Seinfeld* writer Dan O'Keefe who was patient enough to answer my questions. He took the time to read an early draft of the book, and then offered his endorsement. There can never be anyone more knowledgeable about all aspects of Festivus. His help was unparalleled. Don't let the George Costanza act fool you... nobody appreciates the strange magic of Festivus more than DanO.

Thank you to my family, especially my sisters Celeste, Dolores, Marie, Renee, and their families who have celebrated Festivus with me every year since 2005. You all understand Festivus. It was originally Renee's idea, but everyone went along willingly. I could not ask for a better family, including all other family members who cannot be at our yearly Festivus gathering.

A big thank you to test-readers Bettina Allen and Linda Fox who apparently had nothing better to do than read this crappy book. I would also like to extend a special thank you to Lynn Gibson who listened to every one of my lame Festivus musings, even though she is not a Seinfeldist. She then took the time to review and edit my manuscript and helped with the proofing process. She's the best!

About the Author

Mark Nelson's Festivus knowledge has been quoted in national media such as the *Los Angeles Times* and *USA Today*. You may have heard him speak about Festivus on your local radio station such as Kenosha KLIP, WCBS National Radio and KSRO Sonoma. He has a great radio voice, like a cross between James Earl Jones... and Mr. Furley from *Three's Company*. He is one of about 350,000 *Seinfeld* fans living in Winnipeg, Canada. Webmaster of FestivusWeb.com in his off-hours, he spends his days working at Red River College in Winnipeg. He would probably go on strike for a bagel, and often contemplates how cold cuts should be sliced thin so the flavor has nowhere to hide. His ultimate idea of comfort is to be ensconced in velvet and eating a block of cheese the size of a car battery.

More information about this book

- **Web**: festivusweb.com/festivusbook
- **Facebook**: facebook.com/festivusbook
- **Twitter**: twitter.com/festivusbook

How to contact the author

- **Web**: festivusweb.com
- **Twitter**: twitter.com/festivusweb
- **Facebook**: facebook.com/ICelebrateFestivus

Additional titles by Mark Nelson

- *Whiskey 601* (2015) (Fiction)
- *Jackspeak of the Royal Canadian Navy: A Glossary of Canadian Naval Terminology* (2014) (Non-fiction)
- *Winnipeg's Navy: The History of the Naval Reserve in Winnipeg, 1923-2003* (2003) (Non-fiction)

Made in the USA
San Bernardino, CA
22 December 2016